MW01259785

Chicken Burrito Soup, page 48

SOUPified: Soups Inspired by Your Favorite Dishes

31 Innovative Recipes That Ditch the Dish and Embrace the Bowl

by

Michele Di Pietro

Foreword by Mary Giuliani

SOUPified: Soups Inspired by Your Favorite Dishes
31 Innovative Recipes That Ditch the Dish and Embrace the Bowl

ISBN: 978-1-0879-2018-4

Designer: Lizanne Hart
Photographer: Michele Di Pietro
Food and Prop Stylist: Michele Di Pietro

SOUPIFIED is a trademark of It's All About The Food LLC.

www.MangiaWithMichele.com

Cover: Bacon Cheeseburger Soup, page 60

This book is dedicated to my parents, Marguerite and Ozzie, both Italian Americans, who nurtured my love of cooking and giving of myself though food.

Fortunately, they didn't disown me when I told them that I didn't want to be a Certified Public Accountant anymore and wanted to go to cooking school.

SOUPify

[**soop**-*uh*-fahy]

verb (used with object), SOUP·i·fied, SOUP·i·fy·ing.
to make into soup; make liquid and able to be eaten with a spoon:
to SOUPify your favorite dish.

OTHER WORDS FROM SOUPify
SOUP·i·fi·ca·tion, noun: the act of SOUPifying
SOUP·i·fied, adjective: made into soup
SOUP·i·fi·er, SOUP·i·fi·ca·tor, noun: person who SOUPifies

table of contents

Clams Casino Soup, page 28

foreword

"Her recipes make you say 'I'll try' rather than 'I can't.'" –Mary Giuliani

Twenty years ago, when I ditched my fancy diploma for a career in food, my loving and over-protective Italian American parents did not get mad or roll their eyes. Instead, my father simply repeated a mantra to me that he had followed for his own career path: "If you do what you love, you'll never work a day in your life." Years later, after I had achieved what my alma mater declared "a success" in my industry, I was asked to sit on a panel of other HoyaPreneurs (graduates of Georgetown University who also decided to ride this bumpy but beautiful road into the world of kitchen and culinary arts). When I found myself seated next to Michele at this gathering of "Foodie Hoyas," it was if I had found my long-lost foodie sister. And while both of us have careened through food career pivots and ups and downs, Michele and I always lovingly discussed our collective histories—how we came from the same type of home, where food was not a trend or a fad. Rather, it was love, and in many ways, a way of life. It was how you gathered and bonded with your family. The kitchen was not a place to perfect your skills or show off, but rather a place to share your heart by singing, laughing, crying (come on, we're Italian), all the while making a meal that was often simple but oh so special.

Michele has been able to pull off something remarkable with this book (beyond the genius that is her Garlic Bread Soup and Chicken Scarpariello Soup). She has come up with something unique in an often crowded space by introducing us to her creative, delicious, and heartwarming recipes, all written during quarantine; a time when we all longed to be in those big Italian kitchens listening to Dean Martin and hearing our grandfathers laugh. She truly wrote (and cooked) this book with her heart. Each recipe has a touch of humor, whimsy, and best of all, inclusion—they are approachable and fun and make you feel like you can actually pull off something delicious in any type of kitchen. Her recipes make you say "I'll try" rather than "I can't." I fell in love with Michele immediately that day, when the culinary gods placed us side by side on that panel discussion, and you will too after reading and cooking up a pot of her wonderful soups. I have been *SOUPified*, as will you. Brava to Michele on this joyful, delicious collection.

MARY GIULIANI is the author of *Tiny Hot Dogs: A Memoir in Small Bites* and *The Cocktail Party: Eat Drink Play Recover;* a Lifestyle and Party Expert; and CEO of Mary Giuliani Catering and Events.

introduction | *SOUPified:* The Inspiration for a Cookbook

I once read that every good soup tells a story. So true!

These soups *definitely* tell a story.

They were born out of the quarantine period of the COVID-19 pandemic, when I spent countless days being cooped up in a one-bedroom, New York City apartment with no outdoor space and a lot of extra time on my hands. I needed to focus on something positive, challenging, and delicious. I began by transforming a handful of favorite dishes into soup versions, or, in my parlance, I *SOUPified* them. My desire soon grew into a full cookbook of *SOUPified* recipes—which has never been done before.

While this cookbook is an original concept, I will never forget what one of my favorite chef instructors, Chef Scanlan, told us our first week in culinary school. He looked at all of us wide-eyed students in our pristine chef whites and waved his finger at us saying, "None of you will ever develop anything new or original. It has all been done before." He believed that as culinary students, we needed to learn proper cooking techniques and become great cooks first. And even after mastering our culinary skills, we would still only ever be putting our particular spin on something that had already been created.

For the most part, I agree with Chef Scanlan. But, that doesn't make our cooking any less special or delicious. It is unique because *we* made it. Because *we* put our own special twist on it. Because *we* seasoned it. Because of *who we* made it for. Because we put a little bit of ourselves into it and, therefore, made it *our own*.

To Chef Scanlan's point, these soups are inspired by classic dishes—favorites invented years before I came along. My intention was to add my own twist to transform these dishes into a spoonable, bowl form, while holding true to their core soul and spirit. These soups are here to encourage you to look at things in a different way, to think outside the box, and to embrace new, unlikely combinations.

These thirty-one recipes are the weekend comfort food soups of your dreams—hearty compilations of flavor, color, and texture, many of which are meals in and of themselves. They are intended to bring people together around the cutting board, stove, and of course, the table. Whimsical and fun, they are meant to be shared!

my soupified journey

There are so many things that inspire the foods that I create and the way that I cook. It all began with my childhood full of home cooking as an Italian American. Next came my travels and food-filled journeys, followed by my formal culinary education and years working as a chef. But quite honestly, my passion for eating great-tasting food may be what has influenced my cooking the most.

My biggest satisfaction, by far, comes from seeing people's faces when they enjoy my food— that moment of utter silence around the table after their first bite. This is what drives me and brings me joy. This is my true inspiration.

These recipes represent my desire to keep things interesting in the kitchen and continually evolve. They are my tribute to the people and traditions that created the originals. They represent my desire to inspire boundless cooking in you.

I hope that you love and enjoy *SOUPified* as much as I loved creating it. So, please, grab your apron, turn the page, ditch the dish, and embrace the bowl! And ask yourself—what could I *SOUPify* today?

getting started | Preparing to *SOUPify*

Equipment

You really don't need a kitchen full of equipment to make soups successfully. The pieces that you do need, however, are key, and you're likely to use them over and over once you get addicted to making soups from scratch!

In addition to a modest bowl and spoon to enjoy your creation (and let's face it, a large mug will do the job!), here are some tips about what to have on hand to make your *SOUPifying* seamless.

soup pots

I call for a 6.5-quart or larger pot or Dutch oven in all of the recipes for hot soups in this book. That is definitely bigger than what you will need to hold the actual volume of soup being made, but it gives you plenty of room to stir, whisk, and purée using an immersion blender (more on this below). As in cooking pasta, I believe in giving yourself lots of room to cook and not overcrowding the pot or pan. It's easier and more pleasant.

I developed every one of the hot soups in this book in my 7.5-quart, enamel-coated cast iron Dutch oven, and it was perfect. I love cooking with enamel-coated cast iron because it has some non-stick properties, doesn't require seasoning, and is easy to clean. However, a cast-iron Dutch oven is by no means required. Just be sure to use a pot with a thick, heavy bottom. Otherwise, the soup may burn if you don't stir it constantly. The heavy-gauge aluminum pots that you can find in restaurant supply stores are relatively inexpensive and never disappoint. If you're staying away from aluminum, though, a good stainless steel pot is always a wise choice.

It's also a good idea to have soup pots in a variety of sizes for when you want to make only a half-batch or smaller of a particular recipe.

immersion blender

Also known as a hand blender or a hand-held blender, an immersion blender is indispensable for soup makers! You immerse it directly into a pot of liquid for puréeing soft ingredients. There's no need to transfer a hot soup to a blender or food processor and risk spills, burns, and messes. Along with my garlic slicer, my citrus juicer, and my zester/grater, my immersion blender is one of my favorite kitchen tools! They come in all sizes and prices, but there is no need to splurge on something fancy. Just be sure to buy one with a plastic guard on the bottom so that it won't damage the surface of a nonstick pan or enamel-coated Dutch oven.

You will need an immersion blender for several of the recipes in this book. While you can use a blender or food processor as an alternative in a pinch, you will become accustomed to the ease, convenience, and speed of this hand-held equipment. Trust me.

A few tips when using an immersion blender include:

• Immerse it in the liquid before turning it on.

• Keep it moving for best results and do not hold it steady in one place. Immersion blenders do their best work when moved around and tilted while blending. This helps the blender to pick up all ingredients and purée evenly.

• Some people prefer to let hot dishes cool completely before blending (due to the fear of occasional hot splatters). This is up to you, but I promise that your comfort blending with the immersion blender will grow with each use.

If you don't have access to an immersion blender and still want to make one of the puréed soups in this book, you can! Just cool the soup a bit first, and then carefully ladle a few cups of soup at a time into a blender or food processor and blend. Be sure to work in small batches (in other words, fill the appliance only halfway) to keep the soup from splattering or exploding in the blender or food processor, and be sure the lid is firmly in place and secure before you power it on. I do not recommend removing the center of the lid when puréeing hot items.

food processor

While I recommend an immersion blender to purée several of the hot soups in this book, a reliable food processor is the best option for puréeing the cold soups. If you are new to food processors, I'm sure you'll find that it will quickly become an important part of your culinary arsenal and one that you'll use rather often. Whether you're making dips, pesto, or dressings, you will find that it's versatile and easy to use. Many food processors these days come with optional attachments to make slicing, shredding, and dicing seamless. I suggest a processor with a bowl holding 11 cups or more.

miscellaneous tools and equipment

BOWLS: While it's not absolutely necessary, having an assortment of bowls in different sizes will help you organize and hold prepped soup ingredients. Plus, it will make you feel satisfied when you see all of your prep (also called *mise en place*) laid out in front of you in bowls.

BOX GRATER: This four-sided device for grating foods has a different type of grating surface on each side. Use the large teardrop holes to shred soft cheeses, such as cheddar and Swiss cheeses, cabbage, or carrots, and the side that looks like it's covered in round little stars for hard cheeses like Pecorino Romano and Parmigiano-Reggiano.

LADLE: A collection of different-sized ladles is helpful for making and serving soup. However, if you can have only one size, I suggest a 6- to 8-ounce ladle, as it's the most versatile.

KNIVES: Nothing will replace a good set of knives. If you are going to splurge in one area, this is the place to do it. Equipping yourself with the proper knives is key—I have used the same knives for more than 20 years, and they are still going strong. But don't feel that you have to buy lots of knives. An 8- to 10-inch chef's knife, a 3½-inch paring knife, and a serrated (jagged-edged) knife will handle almost any task in your kitchen. Just be sure to keep them sharp! If you don't have a sharpening stone or tool, be sure to get them professionally sharpened. You are more likely to injure yourself using a dull knife than a sharp knife!

MEASURING CUPS and SPOONS: These are a must-have for all *SOUPified* recipes. Become best friends with them. Use a pourable measuring cup for broths and other liquids for convenience.

PARCHMENT PAPER: Use this grease- and moisture-resistant paper that is specially treated for oven use to line sheet pans when you're roasting some of the toppings in this book. Not only do they make the sheet pan non-stick, they make cleanup a breeze!

RUBBER SPATULA: These are useful for getting every last bit of soup out of a pot or food processor, all the tomato paste and beans out of a can, and all the cake batter out of a stand mixer (okay, not relevant to soups, but still). Just don't leave a rubber spatula in a pot of hot soup for too long as it may melt and leave specks of plastic in the soup. Also, the oil and fats in a soup tend to cling to the rubber, causing a stale odor that is impossible to remove.

SCALE: I completely acknowledge and understand that most home cooks do not have or desire a food scale. I am here to say that it is a good idea to have one. While not needed for this particular set of recipes (most of the ingredients in this book are specified in traditional measuring cups and spoons), a scale is a great tool to have in your collection, especially if you like to bake. I have a digital scale that weighs in both imperial and metric. I love it.

SHEET PANS and SKILLETS: You'll need both sheet pans and small and large skillets for the various breadcrumbs, croutons, and other delicious toppings found throughout the recipes in this book. My choice is always stainless steel, but any aluminum or cast iron pan will do.

SPOONS and TONGS: You'll need spoons of all types and shapes and sizes during cooking, whether for tasting, scooping roasted eggplant out of its skin, or adding ingredients to a pot or pan. Keep a slotted spoon on hand to transfer items like crispy bacon and pancetta from the pot to paper towels to drain. Tongs are great for moving larger pieces of food around, such as removing seared chicken breast or thighs from the pot.

STRAINER: Use stainless steel, fine-mesh strainers, large or small, to strain and rinse ingredients such as canned beans, chopped clams, and bean sprouts, or to strain the seeds from freshly squeezed lime or lemon juice.

VEGETABLE PEELER and ZESTER: These are important tools of the trade! You'll need both tools for the recipes throughout the book for prepping potatoes, carrots, lemons, limes, and more.

WHISK: I suggest having one large and one small whisk. You'll need them when adding ingredients like cheese, cream, or miso to the soups.

WOODEN SPOONS: I have more wooden spoons in more shapes and sizes than I will ever need! Yet somehow, they all seem to get used at some point. Wooden spoons are my go-to tool for mixing and scraping all the brown bits from the bottom of any pot or pan. I prefer them over metal spoons, which tend to scrape against the bottom of the pot and become too hot to hold if you leave them in a hot pot for too long.

Notes About the Recipes

yields and serving sizes

All of the soups in this book make either 4 to 6 or 6 to 8 servings. For hot soups, which are absolutely meals in and of themselves, a serving size is considered about 2 cups. For cold soups, which you can serve as starters or accompaniments to a light meal, a serving size is considered 1 cup.

These recipes make a big pot of soup! They are meant to be enjoyed in groups or shared with others. They are designed to have some leftovers—which I promise you will be happy about. Embrace and enjoy the abundance!

Nevertheless, sometimes you may want to make a smaller batch. All of these recipes can be cut in half or quartered—as you wish!

toppings

Lots of the recipes in this book have really delicious toppings, such as croutons, toasted breadcrumbs, and fried bits, built into the ingredients and procedures. These toppings are key to *SOUPification* and provide the textures and flavor experiences that may otherwise get "lost in translation" when the underlying dish is *SOUPified*. They help to bring out the spirit of the original dish on which the soup recipe is based.

Consider these toppings an integral part of the recipe. Plus, they're just plain fun! You might even be tempted to make more than you need to pair them with other dishes. For example, the Pecorino Croutons and Crumbs in Michele's Garlic Bread Soup recipe are divine and perfect on your favorite Caesar salad as well. And the Fried Cheesy Breadcrumbs from the Eggplant Parm Soup recipe are a winner sprinkled over grilled asparagus or *spaghetti aglio e olio* (spaghetti with garlic and oil). Experiment and enjoy—the possibilities are endless! Plus, in most cases, you can make these toppings several hours ahead of time and hold them until you're ready to serve the soup.

As for optional toppings, these are up to you. They complement the overall soup and make it more interesting, but you can leave them out if you wish.

time and temperatures

I've provided approximate cooking times and temperatures for the stovetop and oven, but these will likely vary based on the type and size of pot you are using and your individual equipment. Use them as a guideline and always refer to the other information in the recipe to assist with specifics.

Speaking of guidelines, I use the term "simmer" a lot in this book. This means that you should keep the mixture just below the rapid boiling point of water, when you'll see bubbles forming and gently rising to the surface of the liquid, but the liquid is not yet at a full rolling boil. (Technically, a simmer is between 180 to 205°F.) I feel that soup can be better controlled during the cooking process if you simmer it, as opposed to boiling it. However, if you prefer to bring the soup mixture up to a boil and then turn it down to a simmer, that's up to you. If you're making any soup that contains milk or sour cream, do not bring it up to a boil after you add these ingredients, as they tend to curdle and break.

ingredients

For the most part, the ingredients in these recipes are common, everyday ingredients with which you are probably already familiar. However, a few might be new to you and need a bit more explanation. Here is some additional information and clarification:

BROTH: The quality of the broth or stock that you use in these recipes is super-important! Homemade stock or broth is always the best option, as it is generally fresher, better tasting, cleaner, and less salty than any store-bought variety. However, we all don't have the time or space to consistently have homemade broth on hand, so purchased broth is absolutely acceptable. I only advise that you purchase

one with as few ingredients as possible and one that is low-sodium or no-sodium, if at all possible. It is always better when you can adjust the amount of salt in any recipe to your own needs and taste.

Speaking of broth, as I mentioned before, these *SOUPified* recipes are hearty and full of different ingredients. Sometimes they are puréed, sometimes they are thick, and other times they are brothy. If you prefer a thinner or more brothy soup than what the recipe makes, feel free to add additional broth as desired. If you prefer a chunkier soup, feel free to skip or reduce the puréeing step.

Find a Basic Homemade Stock recipe on page 110.

SALT: The amount of salt that you add to a recipe should always be to your personal needs and taste. Although I have included an amount as a guideline in every recipe, keep in mind that the particular brand and type of ingredients that you use in the soup will affect its overall sodium level and taste. For example, as mentioned above, I highly recommend you use either no-sodium or low-sodium broth or stock. If, however, you use a different broth, you may not need to add any more salt to the soup. Other ingredients, such as butter, soy sauce, mustard, Worcestershire sauce, and hot sauce, will have the same effect on the overall sodium level of the soup. If you are sensitive to salt, you may prefer just to add it as the last ingredient, to taste.

GARLIC CONFIT: You might be wondering: What is this thing called Garlic Confit in recipes woven throughout this book? Well, it's a magical ingredient that transforms so many dishes. To make it, you cook peeled garlic cloves very slowly over low heat, immersed in a bath of extra-virgin olive oil. The result is a transformed clove—what once was a sharp and spicy note becomes transformed into a sweet, mellow, and earthy tone that has the added benefit of being soft and easily incorporated into the soups presented here.

Why did I include it in so many recipes in this book? It can balance out the more acidic, bitter, and sharper flavors in certain soups, or you might need it to round out a soup's overall flavor. Regardless, it always adds depth and complexity to a recipe. My advice: Make a double or triple batch and let it become a permanent part of your culinary collection. I guarantee that you will find new and exciting uses for it that you never imagined.

Find the Garlic Confit recipe on page 112.

PASTA AND RICE: My goal with the recipes in this book was to make them as streamlined as possible, and that includes using the fewest number of pots and pans necessary. With this in mind, I have incorporated the cooking of any pasta or rice directly into the soup itself, increasing the amount of liquid to accommodate this. If you are accustomed to cooking pasta or rice separately, then adding it to a soup, this approach might appear strange to you. But trust me—it works! However, if you prefer to cook your pasta or rice separately and add them in, that is totally fine. Just reduce the amount of liquid by 1 to 2 cups from what the recipe calls for.

All soup recipes containing pasta in this book refer to the term *al dente*. *Al dente* is an Italian phrase that literally means "to the tooth." It refers to the desired texture of cooked pasta and means that the pasta should have a bit of bite to it and not be mushy and overcooked. Generally, the cooking times noted on a pasta package are meant to achieve a perfect *al dente* texture.

FLOUR: You'll notice that several of the soups in this collection contain flour sprinkled on aromatic vegetables like onions and garlic, after a few minutes of cooking. This is a technique used to thicken the soups, and you could describe it as a "modified" *roux*. A roux is fat and flour cooked together that you can use to thicken sauces, soups, and stews. Traditionally, you would add flour to melted butter or oil and then whisk them together for a few minutes before combining them with other ingredients. By sprinkling flour over vegetables that have already been cooked in fat (whether oil, butter, or both), you are essentially creating a roux through an alternative series of steps. In the long run, it's a great way to keep these recipes streamlined and able to be made in just one pot.

MISO: Miso may seem like a strange ingredient to many people, but it has an important role in each soup in which it appears, adding a large amount of savoriness (also known as *umami*) and flavor that helps to bring out the spirit of the underlying dish on which the soup is based. Miso is a fermented soy paste that's in the refrigerated section of most grocery stores, near the sauerkraut and pickles. It comes in white and red varieties. (Sometimes it is simply labeled as "soybean paste.") Choose white miso for the recipes in this book. If you can't find miso, you can use a low-sodium soy sauce as a substitute. The only drawback is that soy sauce is generally much saltier than miso, so add about half the amount of miso called for, then work your way up from there. For a soy-free option, choose a miso that is made from chickpeas or brown rice.

some general recipe and cooking guidelines

- Read through the entire list of ingredients carefully when planning to make the recipe and be sure to incorporate any ingredients that you don't have on hand into your next shopping list. See the recipe notes at the end of each recipe for possible ingredient substitutions.

- Read through the entire recipe at least once so that you understand all of the cooking steps.

- Always wash your vegetables before prepping them!

- Be aware of potential cross-contamination when it comes to raw shellfish and meats. Keep raw products separate from cooked products, and do not use the same cutting board for raw proteins and cooked ingredients. Otherwise you could sicken yourself and others.

- It is always a great idea to prep all of your

ingredients before getting started. It may be a bit more time up front, but it will save you some potential frustration later on, especially if you have to stop cooking and turn off the heat in order to chop some ingredients that you forgot about.

- Make the soup toppings first and then set them aside until you are ready. You'll be happy you did this!

soup storage, freezing, and reheating

If you are making full batches of the soups in this book, you will likely (and luckily!) have leftovers to enjoy again. Soup is one of the best meals to make ahead and in large batches. You can enjoy it throughout the week and it's great for sharing with neighbors, friends, and family!

To help you manage and work with that extra soup, here are some tips:

STORAGE: After cooling hot soup, transfer it promptly to an airtight container or freezer bag, cover or seal it tightly, and refrigerate or freeze. If properly stored, all of the hot soups in this book should last up to 5 days in the refrigerator and up to 3 months in the freezer. I do not recommend freezing any of the cold soups in this book as it will negatively affect the soups' texture.

FREEZING: I have frozen and later enjoyed every one of the hot soups in this book, as has my sister. People may disagree with me and say that certain types of soups should not be frozen, but you can freeze every one of the hot soup recipes in this book. Most foods, once frozen, will lack some of the luster and unique texture that they have when they are just freshly made. However, I am big on managing my expectations, and so I know this going in. For me, any variance in texture or experience that results from freezing something far outweighs the convenience of having something delicious to eat in a pinch.

Here are some general guidelines about freezing, along with information about the best soups to freeze (or not to freeze), and steps that you can take to make some soups freeze better:

- Choose a freezer-proof container or resealable freezer plastic bag to help prevent freezer burn.

- Consider freezing soup in individual servings for a convenient grab-and-go meal for one.

- Don't fill the container to the top! Liquids expand in the freezer, so leave 1 to 2 inches of space in the storage container or bag to account for this expansion.

- Label it! No matter how often I say that I will remember what's in that container, I rarely do. Do yourself a favor and label the container with the recipe name and the date you made it. Use an erasable marker or masking tape.

- Leave the garnishes off—they won't have the same textural effect once frozen.

- Eat frozen soups within 3 months of freezing.

- Brothy soups without dairy, potatoes, pasta, or rice freeze the best.

- Soups with cream or other dairy (such as sour cream, cheese, or milk) may develop a grainy texture or separate in the freezer or while being reheated. One option is to freeze these soups without the dairy and then add it during the reheating process. Another (easier) option is to slowly thaw a soup with dairy in the refrigerator, which may take 1 to 2 days, then reheat it very slowly over low heat while stirring. You can also consider stirring in some additional fresh cream or milk, if desired.

- Soups with noodles, pasta, or rice are not ideal for freezing as the noodles or rice tend to soak up all the moisture and disintegrate during the freezing process. One option is to prepare the soup without the pasta or rice and freeze only the base of the soup. During reheating, you can prepare the pasta or rice separately and add it to the soup.

- Soups with potatoes are not ideal for freezing. Like pasta or rice, potatoes tend to sponge up any moisture in a soup and can become grainy once defrosted.

REHEATING: When you are ready to reheat the soup, you have a couple of options. If the soup is frozen, you can either thaw it in the refrigerator for 1 to 2 days, thaw it in the microwave, or thaw the soup in a warm-water bath until it loosens from the side of the container or bag, at which point you can then transfer the soup (which might still be an ice block) into a large saucepan.

Since non-brothy soups tend to become thicker during refrigerated or frozen storage, you will likely need to add a little broth or water to the saucepan while reheating until the soup reaches the desired consistency. Slowly heat thicker soups, especially those containing dairy, over low or medium-low heat, stirring frequently, until hot. Boiling may cause the dairy products to separate or curdle. Therefore, I do not recommend defrosting soups with dairy in a microwave.

Heat broth-based soups in a saucepan over medium heat, stirring occasionally, until hot, or reheat in the microwave.

Elote (Mexican Street Corn) Soup, page 14

vegetarian *soups*

eggplant parm soup | *Serves 6 to 8*

Back when I was in cooking school, I was briefly interviewed by the local news for a quick segment about a topic that I cannot recall — what I remember is that I was unbelievably nervous to be interviewed and to be on TV. In fact, I had to do so many re-takes because I kept laughing when I answered. Why was I laughing? Well, as I said, I was super-nervous. But, the newsperson also had a huge red lipstick stain on her teeth that I could not unsee, and she was only a couple of inches from my face. Hey, I did the best I could. At the end of the interview, she asked me what my favorite dish was and I blurted out without thinking "my mom's eggplant parmesan"! It was not a very cheffy answer; I didn't say steak au poivre or sole meunière or beef bourguignon, as many culinary students would have said at that point. No, at that moment of nervous laughter in a very uncomfortable situation, the first thing that I thought of was something that clearly meant pure comfort to me.

Years later, it still does. And, it always will. How I yearn for my mom's eggplant parm — a dish that she made time and time again for our family with more love than an army of professional chefs.

I am thrilled to make this my first recipe in my first cookbook. This is my mom's eggplant parm through and through—crispy, breaded layers of very thinly sliced eggplant, melted mozzarella cheese, and sweet tomato sauce—in soup form. I hope you love it as much as I do.

ingredients

2 large eggplants, rinsed and patted dry (about 2 ½ to 3 pounds)

¼ cup olive oil

2 cups diced yellow onions (about 1 medium onion)

3 cups lightly packed fresh basil leaves, roughly chopped, divided

¼ cup chopped garlic (9 to 10 cloves)

¼ teaspoon crushed red pepper

¼ cup tomato paste

6 cups low-sodium vegetable or chicken broth

1 can (14.5 ounces) whole, diced, or crushed tomatoes

1 teaspoon salt

½ teaspoon black pepper

3 cups shredded mozzarella (about 12 ounces)

⅓ cup grated Pecorino Romano cheese

1 recipe Fried Cheesy Breadcrumbs (page 4)

instructions

1 Prepare Fried Cheesy Breadcrumbs and set aside.

2 Roast eggplant: Arrange rack in middle of oven and preheat to 350°F. Using tip of a sharp knife or prongs of a fork, make 2 to 3 slits in each eggplant, then place eggplants on a wire rack, set atop a sheet pan. (You can also bake them directly on a parchment-lined sheet pan.) Place sheet pan on middle oven rack and bake until eggplants are very tender and their skin is wrinkly (45 to 60 minutes). Test eggplants' doneness by inserting a knife through its thickest part; it should not meet with any resistance in its center. Use tongs to remove eggplant to a cutting board or wire rack and let it cool. Once cool enough to handle, cut off and discard its stem and slice eggplant in half. Use a large spoon to carefully scoop out

and set aside all of the cooked eggplant flesh. *(NOTE: This can be done one to two days in advance and held in an airtight container in the refrigerator.)* Discard eggplant skins.

3 Heat oil in 6-quart (or larger) pot or Dutch oven over medium heat. Add onions, 1½ cups basil, garlic, and crushed red pepper and cook for about 4 minutes, or until onions have softened a bit, stirring occasionally.

4 Move onion mixture to one side of pot, then add tomato paste and cook it for about 30 seconds. Add 2 cups broth and stir to loosen and scrape up any browned bits on the bottom of the pot.

5 Add remaining broth, tomatoes, salt, black pepper, and reserved eggplant pulp. Mix until all ingredients are well combined. Cover pot and bring mixture to a simmer, stirring occasionally. Simmer, uncovered, for about 15 to 18 minutes, stirring regularly.

6 Reduce heat to low. Then carefully purée mixture until smooth using an immersion blender. Slowly whisk in cheeses, 1 cup at a time, ensuring each cup has melted before adding the next. Finish by mixing in remaining 1½ cups basil, then turn off heat.

7 Ladle soup into bowls and top with Fried Cheesy Breadcrumbs.

recipe notes

- If you are sensitive to eggplant seeds, remove those as best as possible after cooking the eggplant. They don't bother most people, but some eggplants have more (and larger) seeds than others, and they often do not break down after the puréeing step. The round and smaller eggplant varieties have fewer seeds.

- In this case, it is better to overcook, rather than undercook, the eggplant. If the eggplant pulp is not fully cooked and soft, it will be very difficult to scrape it out from the skins.

fried cheesy breadcrumbs

4 tablespoons olive oil
1 cup plain breadcrumbs
¼ cup grated Pecorino Romano cheese
¼ cup grated Parmigiano-Reggiano cheese
¼ teaspoon salt
¼ teaspoon black pepper
¼ teaspoon dried oregano

Heat oil in small skillet over medium-low heat. Add breadcrumbs, cheeses, and spices and cook until breadcrumbs are toasted, about 2 to 3 minutes, stirring continuously. Remove from heat and set aside, uncovered, at room temperature.

You can make these breadcrumbs 3 to 4 hours in advance and hold them, uncovered, at room temperature.

cavatelli with broccoli soup | *Serves 4 to 6*

Cavatelli (a small, curled pasta) with broccoli is a staple in any Italian American kitchen. It is perfect in its simplicity and laser-focused on its few main flavors—broccoli (which is often overcooked until it can be smashed with a fork), garlic, Pecorino Romano cheese, and lots of extra-virgin olive oil. Like a good chicken soup, it seems to be a cure-all for many.

Here, you can achieve that same fork-smashed quality of the soft broccoli hugging the cavatelli pieces when you purée the soup with some hearty cannellini beans. Mellow Garlic Confit, a splash of miso, and a bit of lemon round out the flavors, adding a decidedly savory and bright finish to an already beautiful flavor combination.

ingredients

¼ cup olive oil

2 cups diced yellow onions (about 1 medium onion)

½ cup chopped garlic (18 to 20 cloves)

½ teaspoon crushed red pepper

½ cup dry white wine, such as pinot grigio

7 cups low-sodium vegetable or chicken broth

1½ pounds fresh or frozen broccoli florets, large pieces cut in half

1 cup cooked cannellini beans, drained and rinsed if from a can

¼ cup Garlic Confit cloves (page 112)

½ teaspoon salt

¼ teaspoon black pepper

12 ounces fresh or 10 ounces dried cavatelli or other small pasta such as orecchiette or malloreddus pasta (about 2 cups)

3 tablespoons white miso

1 cup finely grated Pecorino Romano cheese

6 tablespoons fresh lemon juice (zest lemons first)

1 tablespoon lemon zest

Lemon oil (optional topping)

instructions

1 Prepare Garlic Confit if you do not have any on hand.

2 Heat oil in 6-quart (or larger) pot or Dutch oven over medium heat. Add onions, garlic, and crushed red pepper and cook for about 4 minutes, or until onions have softened a bit, stirring occasionally.

3 Add wine and stir to loosen and scrape up any browned bits on bottom of pot.

4 Add broth, broccoli, beans, Garlic Confit, salt, and black pepper, and mix until all ingredients are well combined. Cover pot and bring mixture to a simmer, stirring occasionally. Simmer until broccoli is soft enough to purée (about 10 minutes).

5 Reduce heat to low. Then carefully purée mixture until smooth using an immersion

blender. Or, if you prefer a chunkier soup with some pieces of broccoli, only partially purée mixture.

6 Increase heat and return mixture to a boil, then stir in cavatelli. Cook pasta, uncovered, while stirring frequently so that it does not stick or get clumpy. The amount of liquid needed may vary based on whether you use fresh or dried cavatelli. Adjust this as needed and to your personal taste regarding how thick you would like the soup. For example, add additional broth or water to soup if it is too thick.

7 When pasta is *al dente,* whisk in miso and stir until well combined. Turn off heat. Then add cheese, lemon juice, and lemon zest and stir until cheese has melted.

8 Ladle soup into bowls and top with lemon oil, if desired.

recipe notes

- If you are unable to find miso, you can use 1½ tablespoons low-sodium soy sauce.

- Be sure to zest the limes before squeezing out their juice!

michele's garlic bread soup | *Serves 4 to 6*

This soup is super-personal to me. I know—it's based on garlic bread, so how personal can it be? But, you see, my garlic bread is known widely throughout my circle. In fact, it is the item my family and friends most often request.

This soup is not for the faint of heart! Having said this, although it contains a fair amount of raw garlic, the softer and more mellow flavor of the Garlic Confit balances it well. It is delicious on its own, but I would be remiss if I didn't state that the croutons make this soup! In fact, these may just be the world's best croutons. My suggestion? Double, even triple, the batch of croutons, as you will surely want to add them to everything, or just pop them directly into your mouth!

ingredients

2 tablespoons unsalted butter

2 tablespoons olive oil or Garlic Oil (page 112)

2 cups diced shallots (about 4 shallots)

1 cup diced celery (about 3 to 4 ribs)

¼ cup finely minced garlic (9 to 10 cloves)

2 tablespoons chopped fresh flat-leaf parsley

½ cup dry white wine, such as pinot grigio

¼ cup red wine vinegar

2 tablespoons sherry vinegar

6 cups low-sodium vegetable or chicken broth

¾ cup Garlic Confit cloves (page 112)

1¼ teaspoons salt

1 teaspoon dried thyme

¼ teaspoon black pepper

2 bay leaves

5 cups day-old Italian bread cut into 1 to 2-inch pieces

½ cup heavy cream

¼ cup finely grated Pecorino Romano cheese

¼ cup finely grated Parmigiano-Reggiano cheese

1 recipe Pecorino Croutons and Crumbs (page 10)

instructions

1 Prepare Garlic Oil (if using) and Garlic Confit if you do not have any on hand.

2 Prepare Pecorino Croutons and Crumbs and set aside.

3 Heat butter and oil in 6-quart (or larger) pot or Dutch oven over medium-high heat. When butter has melted, add shallots, celery, garlic, and parsley. Cook, covered, for about 4 minutes or until vegetables have softened a bit, stirring occasionally.

4 Add wine and vinegars. Stir to loosen and scrape up any browned bits on bottom of pot.

5 Add broth, Garlic Confit, salt, thyme, black pepper, and bay leaves. Mix until all ingredients are well combined. Cover pot and bring mixture to a simmer, stirring occasionally.

Simmer, covered, for 15 minutes, stirring regularly.

6 Remove bay leaves. Then stir in bread and heavy cream. Reduce heat to low. Then carefully purée mixture until smooth using an immersion blender. Turn off heat, add cheeses, and purée again until smooth.

7 Ladle soup into bowls and top with Pecorino Croutons and Crumbs.

recipe notes

- Grana Padano cheese is a great substitute for the Parmigiano-Reggiano.

- Use a high-quality granulated garlic or garlic powder in this recipe—it makes a difference!

pecorino croutons and crumbs

¼ cup finely grated Pecorino Romano cheese
¼ cup finely grated Parmigiano-Reggiano cheese
¼ cup finely chopped fresh flat-leaf parsley
1 teaspoon granulated garlic or garlic powder
1 teaspoon freshly ground black pepper
½ cup olive oil
4 to 5 cups day-old Italian bread cut into ¾ to 1-inch cubes (about 4 to 5 slices)

Mix cheeses, parsley, garlic, and pepper together in large bowl. Set aside.

Heat oil in large skillet over medium heat. Add bread cubes, toss with oil to coat, then spread them out into a single layer in skillet. Brown bread cubes, rotating and browning on multiple sides. Do this in batches, if necessary.

Transfer crispy fried bread to bowl with the cheese mixture. Toss quickly so that croutons are well coated in mixture. Then, place croutons on a paper towel in a single layer to drain. Be sure to save leftover Pecorino "crumbs" for soup topping as well.

You can make these croutons 3 to 4 hours in advance and hold them, uncovered, at room temperature.

spinach quiche soup | *Serves 4 to 6*

My Sicilian-American mom always made a killer spinach quiche. What I loved the most about it was that it was jam-packed with spinach filling, containing only enough custard to hold it all together. It was creamy and earthy, with lots of Gruyère and Swiss cheeses, and it had just the right amount of onion crunch to round everything out.

This soup is based on that delicious memory. It's akin to a creamy spinach soup with more dimension. Those typical spinach quiche flavors come to the surface through a little Dijon mustard, a little Worcestershire sauce, and a lot of savory pie crust crumbled over the whole thing. Don't leave the Pie Crust Topping out—you'll miss it!

ingredients

4 tablespoons unsalted butter

2 cups diced yellow onion (about 1 medium onion)

¼ cup chopped garlic (9 to 10 cloves)

5 tablespoons all-purpose flour

4 cups low-sodium vegetable or chicken broth

3 cups whole milk

3 packages (10 ounces) frozen chopped spinach, thawed and liquid squeezed out

5 teaspoons Worcestershire sauce

4 teaspoons hot sauce

4 teaspoons Dijon-style mustard

1½ teaspoons black pepper

1 teaspoon salt

¼ cup heavy cream

8 ounces Swiss cheese, shredded or cut into very small pieces

8 ounces Gruyère cheese, shredded or cut into very small pieces

1 cup grated Pecorino Romano cheese

¼ cup chopped green onion (about 1 onion)

1 recipe Pie Crust Topping (page 13)

instructions

1 Prepare Pie Crust Topping and set aside.

2 Melt butter in 6-quart (or larger) pot or Dutch oven over medium heat. Add onions and garlic and cook for about 4 minutes, or until onions have softened a bit, stirring occasionally.

3 Sprinkle flour on top of onion mixture. Stir to coat and continue stirring for 1 to 2 minutes while flour cooks. Gradually pour in 2 cups broth and whisk mixture quickly to fully incorporate flour into liquid until smooth. Then stir to loosen and scrape up any browned bits on bottom of pot.

4 Add remaining broth, milk, spinach, Worcestershire and hot sauces, mustard, black pepper, and salt. Mix until all ingredients are well combined. Then cover pot and bring mixture to a simmer. Simmer,

uncovered, for about 10 to 12 minutes, or until all vegetables have softened, stirring occasionally to prevent sticking. Reduce heat, if necessary, to maintain a simmer.

5 Turn heat to low, then whisk in cream. Gradually stir in cheeses, 1 cup at a time, ensuring each cup has melted before adding the next. Finish by stirring in green onions, then turn off heat.

6 Ladle soup into bowls and top with Pie Crust Topping.

recipe notes

- You can defrost the spinach either at room temperature or by heating it on the stove or in the microwave. Just be sure to squeeze out excess liquid before adding to broth.

- If you prefer to use fresh spinach, blanch it for 20 seconds in boiling water. Then remove it with a colander and run it under cold water. Squeeze out all excess liquid, then chop it into bite-sized pieces.

pie crust topping

1 (9-inch) frozen pie shell, unbaked
Pinch coarse salt, black pepper, and garlic powder

Place frozen pie shell (in its original pan) on sheet pan and let it sit at room temperature for about 15 minutes.

Sprinkle it liberally with the spices, then prick shell in several places with a fork. Follow instructions on package for an unfilled crust or bake it at 375°F for about 12 minutes, or until it has browned a bit.

Remove and let cool, then break into random smaller pieces to use as soup topping. Set aside, uncovered, at room temperature.

You can make this topping 3 to 4 hours in advance and hold it, uncovered, at room temperature.

elote (mexican street corn) soup | *Serves 4 to 6*

I first had elote at an outdoor food festival in Brooklyn about 10 years ago and was immediately hooked. It's a Mexican version of corn on the cob that has been charred on the grill, then slathered in a spicy mayo cream sauce and sprinkled (generously) with chili powder, cheese, and lime. It is street food in its best, most fun, and messy form. Grilling the shucked ears of corn brings out its natural nutty flavor and the spicy and savory flavors that are paired with it makes the corn sweet, salty, creamy and tart all at once.

This SOUPified version of Mexican street corn is a lot less messy than the original, but it lacks none of its magic. Get some sweet summer corn, cut it off its cob, and then sauté it in butter and oil until brown to bring out its nuttiness. Then add the cobs back into the broth to increase the soup's beautiful corn flavor. Aromatics and some heat make this pure street eats in spoonable soup form.

ingredients

2 tablespoons olive oil

2 tablespoons unsalted butter

5 ears of fresh corn, kernels cut off cob and silk removed (about 4 cups kernels), stripped corncobs reserved for broth

2 cups diced yellow onions (about 1 medium onion)

1 cup diced celery (about 3 to 4 ribs)

1 poblano pepper, seeded, stemmed, and finely chopped (include seeds if you prefer more heat!)

¼ cup chopped garlic (9 to 10 cloves)

3 cups low-sodium vegetable or chicken broth

3 cups whole milk

1 pound Yukon gold or other waxy potatoes cut into 1-inch pieces, held in cold water to prevent browning

2 bay leaves

2 teaspoons salt

1½ teaspoons dried Mexican or regular oregano

½ teaspoon chili powder

½ teaspoon chipotle chili powder

¼ teaspoon black pepper

1 cup crumbled cotija or feta cheese

1 cup Mexican *crema* or sour cream

½ cup fresh lime juice (zest limes first)

¼ cup chopped cilantro

1 tablespoon lime zest

instructions

1 Brown corn: Heat oil and butter in 6-quart (or larger) pot or Dutch oven over medium-high heat. When butter has melted, add corn kernels and cook until they start to brown (about 5 to 7 minutes), stirring occasionally. Do this in batches if necessary. Then remove about ⅔ of corn with a slotted spoon and set aside.

2 Add onions, celery, poblano pepper, and garlic. Cook for about 4 minutes, or until vegetables have softened, stirring occasionally.

3 Add broth and stir to loosen and scrape up any browned bits on bottom of pot.

4 Add milk, potatoes (drain first if being held in water), bay leaves, salt, oregano, chili powders, black pepper, and reserved corncobs.

Stir until all ingredients are well combined. Cover pot and bring mixture to a simmer. Then partially cover and lightly simmer soup until potatoes are tender, stirring frequently (about 20 to 30 minutes).

5 Remove and discard cobs and bay leaves. Reduce heat to low. Then carefully purée mixture until smooth using an immersion blender. Only partially purée soup if you prefer a chunkier version.

6 Add cheese, *crema* or sour cream, lime juice, cilantro, lime zest, and most of reserved sautéed corn kernels, reserving some to use as topping. Stir until all ingredients are well combined. Turn off heat. Do not boil soup once *crema* or sour cream is added to prevent curdling.

7 Ladle soup into bowls and top with remaining cooked corn kernels.

recipe notes

- Although this soup is best with the seasonal sweet corn of summer and early fall, you can absolutely use frozen corn. Just choose a product with the label "yellow sweet corn" and thaw it before using. You will need about 1¼ pounds of corn kernels.

- Different brands of chili powder vary in their level of heat. If you are sensitive to spicy foods, perhaps start with half of the suggested amount, then increase to taste from there. On the other hand, if you prefer more heat in your foods, include some or all of the seeds from the poblano pepper.

- If you are unable to find chipotle powder, use smoked paprika instead.

- *Cotija* is an aged Mexican cow's milk cheese that is white, firm, dry, and salty, similar to Greek feta cheese. Mexican *crema* is a creamy and slightly tangy condiment that is a bit thicker and richer than American sour cream.

- Be sure to zest the limes before squeezing out their juice!

baba ghanoush soup | *Serves 6 to 8*

Baba ghanoush is one of those perfect flavor combinations that relies more on technique than a long list of ingredients. This signature Mediterranean dip—a simple combination of charred eggplants, tahini (sesame seed paste), garlic, lemon juice and extra-virgin olive oil—is simultaneously smoky, sweet, savory, bright, and creamy. It's an all-star eating experience, if you ask me. Traditionally, it starts with eggplants being grilled or broiled over an open flame until their skins are so burnt that you think they might be too far gone to use. This char is what gives baba ghanoush its signature smokiness.

For this SOUPified form, I've taken a more gentle, home-friendly approach to the preparation. Roast the eggplants whole until tender and wrinkled. Then simmer them with some unique ingredients, such as smoked paprika and chipotle chili powder, to lend the soup the additional smokiness it needs. Once you've puréed it and combined it with some fresh lemon juice just before serving, this soup may make you think twice about reaching for a spoon instead of a pita chip.

ingredients

2 large eggplants, rinsed and patted dry (about 2½ to 3 pounds)

¼ cup olive oil, plus more for topping

2 cups diced yellow onion (about 1 medium onion)

7 cups low-sodium vegetable or chicken broth

1 cup roasted red peppers, drained, no seeds (about 8 ounces)

¼ cup Garlic Confit cloves (page 112)

1 tablespoon smoked or regular salt

1 teaspoon black pepper

1 teaspoon ground cumin

½ teaspoon smoked paprika

¼ teaspoon chipotle chili powder

⅓ cup tahini (sesame seed paste)

6 tablespoons fresh lemon juice

½ cup finely chopped fresh parsley (optional topping)

Pinch ground sumac (optional topping)

instructions

1 Prepare Garlic Confit if you do not have any on hand.

2 Roast eggplant: Arrange rack in middle of oven and preheat to 375°F. Using tip of a sharp knife or prongs of a fork, make 2 to 3 slits in each eggplant. Then place eggplants on a wire rack, set atop a sheet pan. (You can also bake them directly on a parchment-lined sheet pan.) Place sheet pan on middle oven rack and bake until eggplants are very tender and their skin is wrinkly (45 to 60 minutes). Test if eggplant is done by inserting a knife through its thickest part; it should not meet with any resistance in its center. Use tongs to remove eggplant to a cutting board or wire rack and let it cool. Once it is cool enough to handle, cut off and discard its stem and slice eggplant in half. Use a large spoon to

carefully scoop out and set aside all of the cooked eggplant pulp. This can be done one to two days in advance, with pulp held in an airtight container in the refrigerator. Discard eggplant skins.

3 Heat oil in 6-quart (or larger) pot or Dutch oven over medium heat. Add onions and cook for about 7 to 8 minutes, or until onions have softened and browned a bit, stirring occasionally.

4 Add 2 cups broth and stir to loosen and scrape up any browned bits on the bottom of pot.

5 Add remaining broth, roasted peppers, Garlic Confit, all spices, and reserved eggplant pulp. Mix until all ingredients are well combined. Cover pot and bring mixture to a simmer, stirring occasionally. Simmer, uncovered, for about 15 to 18 minutes, stirring regularly.

6 Whisk in tahini and lemon juice. Reduce heat to low. Then carefully purée mixture until smooth using an immersion blender. Turn off heat.

7 Ladle soup into bowls, drizzle with a little olive oil, and top with chopped parsley and sumac, if desired.

recipe notes

- If you are sensitive to eggplant seeds, remove those as best as possible after cooking the eggplant. They don't bother most people, but some eggplants have more (and larger) seeds than others, and they often do not break down after the puréeing step. The round and smaller eggplant varieties have fewer seeds.

- In this case, it is better to overcook, rather than undercook, the eggplant. If the eggplant pulp is not fully cooked and soft, it will be very difficult to scrape it out from the skins.

- If you have access to a grill, try grilling the eggplants until charred on all sides instead of roasting them for a more intense, smoky flavor.

- If you are unable to find chipotle (that is, smoked chili) powder, you can use smoked paprika.

- Sumac is a red powdered spice that offers a tart, lemony, and slightly astringent flavor. A little goes a long way, and it is great sprinkled on the Baba Ghanoush Soup!

Crab Cake Soup, page 25

seafood *soups*

shrimp scampi soup | *Serves 6 to 8*

I love a good shrimp scampi. Succulent pieces of shrimp quickly cooked in butter and extra-virgin olive oil with copious amounts of white wine, garlic, and fresh lemon are pretty high on my "Things I Always Want To Eat" list. It turns out that these flavors make a dreamy soup as well!

Here, I rounded out the flavors with some atypical red bell peppers, spinach, and green onions—ingredients that seem to amp up the pleasure factor of the underlying dish exponentially. Pair this soup with some rustic Italian bread and then, all is right in the world.

ingredients

4 tablespoons unsalted butter

4 tablespoons olive oil

½ cup chopped garlic (18 to 20 cloves)

¼ teaspoon crushed red pepper

6 tablespoons all-purpose flour

2 cups dry white wine, such as pinot grigio

8 cups low-sodium vegetable, seafood, or chicken broth

2 tablespoons fork-smashed Garlic Confit cloves (page 112)

1½ teaspoons salt

¼ teaspoon black pepper

2 cups diced red bell pepper (about 2 peppers)

1 cup orzo pasta (7 ounces)

1½ pounds shrimp, peeled, deveined, tail off, cut into bite-sized pieces

3 packed cups chopped fresh baby spinach (about 4 ounces)

¼ cup fresh lemon juice (zest lemons first)

½ cup chopped green onion (about 2 onions)

2 tablespoons chopped fresh flat-leaf parsley, leaves only

1 tablespoon lemon zest

instructions

1 Prepare Garlic Confit if you do not have any on hand.

2 Heat butter and oil in 6-quart (or larger) pot or Dutch oven over medium heat. When butter has melted, add chopped garlic and crushed red pepper. Cook for about 3 minutes, stirring regularly to prevent burning.

3 Sprinkle flour on top of garlic mixture. Stir to coat and continue stirring for 1 to 2 minutes while flour cooks. Gradually pour in wine and whisk mixture quickly to fully incorporate flour into the liquid until smooth. Then stir to loosen and scrape up any browned bits on the bottom of the pot.

4 Add broth, Garlic Confit, salt, and black pepper, and mix until all ingredients are well combined.

5 Cover pot and bring mixture to a simmer, then stir in bell pepper and pasta. Cook pasta, uncovered, while stirring frequently so that it does not stick or get clumpy.

6 When pasta is *al dente,* stir in shrimp, spinach, lemon juice, green onions, parsley, and lemon zest. Continue to simmer until shrimp are fully cooked (about 2 to 3 minutes). Turn off heat.

7 Ladle soup into bowls.

recipe note

- Be sure to zest the lemons before squeezing out their juice!

crab cake soup | *Serves 4 to 6*

Crab cakes have always been one of my favorite foods. Since I grew up in New Jersey and not Maryland (the crab capital of the United States), they were a rare meal for our family and more of a treat than a regular occurrence—perhaps that added to their allure. There is just something about sweet and succulent pieces of lump crab meat mixed with little more than seafood seasoning, egg and mayonnaise then coated in a splash of breadcrumbs and fried.

This soup represents my crab cake experience. While it contains a few outliers that are necessary for the soup format, such as celery, potatoes and bell peppers, the soup's focus is squarely on the crab and the signature crab cake experience and flavors. It's topped with savory and crunchy Chive Breadcrumbs that mimic the seared coating on the classic cakes. Crab cake purist or not, I hope you give this one a try!

ingredients

2 tablespoons unsalted butter

2 tablespoons olive oil

2 cups diced yellow onions (about 1 medium onion)

1 cup diced celery (about 3 to 4 ribs)

¼ cup all-purpose flour

½ cup dry white wine, such as pinot grigio

2½ cups low-sodium vegetable or seafood broth

2½ cups whole milk

1 pound Yukon gold or other waxy potatoes cut into ¼-inch dice, held in cold water to prevent browning

2 tablespoons Dijon-style mustard

4½ teaspoons seafood spice seasoning, such as Old Bay

1 tablespoon Worcestershire sauce

2 teaspoons hot sauce

½ teaspoon salt

¼ teaspoon black pepper

¼ teaspoon cayenne pepper

1½ cups diced bell peppers (about 1½ peppers)

1 pound crab meat, picked for shells

1 recipe Chive Breadcrumbs (page 27)

instructions

1 Prepare Chive Breadcrumbs and set aside.

2 Heat butter and oil in 6-quart (or larger) pot or Dutch oven over medium-high heat. When butter has melted, add onions and celery and cook for about 4 minutes, or until vegetables have softened a bit, stirring occasionally.

3 Sprinkle flour on top of onion mixture. Stir to coat and continue stirring for 1 to 2 minutes while flour cooks. Gradually pour in wine and broth and whisk mixture quickly to fully incorporate flour into the liquid until smooth. Then, stir to loosen and scrape up any browned bits on bottom of pot.

4 Add milk, potatoes (drain first if being held in water), mustard, seafood seasoning, Worcestershire and hot sauces, and spices and stir until well combined. Cover pot and bring mixture to a simmer. Simmer, partially covered, until potatoes are almost cooked, about 15 to 20 minutes, stirring frequently. Add bell peppers and continue to simmer another 3 to 4 minutes.

5 Stir in crabmeat and turn off heat.

6 Ladle soup into bowls and top with Chive Breadcrumbs.

recipe note

- There's no need to use the more expensive lump or jumbo lump crab meat in this soup, unless you really want to. Their signature chunky texture will get lost once mixed with the other ingredients. Backfin or claw crab meat are great options.

chive breadcrumbs

3 tablespoons unsalted butter
½ cup chopped chives
1 cup plain breadcrumbs
¾ teaspoon seafood spice seasoning, such as Old Bay
¼ teaspoon salt
¼ teaspoon black pepper

Melt butter in small skillet over medium heat. Add chives and cook for 1 minute while stirring.

Add remaining breadcrumb ingredients, and mix until all ingredients are well combined. Cook, stirring frequently, until breadcrumbs are toasted (about 2 to 3 minutes). Remove from heat and set aside, uncovered, at room temperature.

You can make these breadcrumbs 3 to 4 hours in advance and hold them, uncovered, at room temperature.

clams casino soup | *Serves 6 to 8*

A staple of New England, clams casino is considered an American classic, and for good reason—it's an inspired pairing of seafood and pork that is chock-full of bacon and buttery breadcrumbs crisped under the broiler. This SOUPified version has all the feel of clams casino and more—shallots, bell peppers, garlic, white wine, and a crispy breadcrumb topping that is toasted in savory bacon fat and full of crispy bacon. Close your eyes and you will swear you are slurping this soup off the half shell.

ingredients

12 ounces bacon cut into ½-inch strips while raw

4 anchovy filets

1 pint grape or cherry tomatoes, quartered

2 cups diced shallots (about 4 shallots)

1 cup diced celery (about 3 to 4 ribs)

1 cup chopped green onions (about 4 onions)

¼ cup chopped garlic (9 to 10 cloves)

¼ cup all-purpose flour

1½ cups dry white wine, such as pinot grigio

7 cups clam juice (4 cups purchased plus 3 cups strained clam juice from the canned clams)

1 pound russet potatoes, peeled and diced, held in cold water to prevent browning

2 cups diced red bell pepper (about 2 peppers)

2 tablespoons hot sauce

½ teaspoon dried thyme

½ teaspoon dried oregano

¼ teaspoon black pepper

6 cans (6.5 ounces) chopped clams in clam juice, strained (Strain and use this clam juice in the soup!)

¼ cup fresh lemon juice (zest lemons first for Breadcrumb recipe)

⅓ cup chopped fresh flat-leaf parsley

1 recipe Crispy Bacon Breadcrumbs (page 30)

instructions

1 Strain clam juice from canned clams as you will need this for the soup. Set aside.

2 Cook bacon: Place bacon in 6-quart (or larger) pot or Dutch oven over medium heat. Slowly cook it until it becomes crispy and most of the fat has been rendered. Remove bacon with a slotted spoon and set it aside to drain on paper towels. Use ½ cup of this cooked bacon in the Crispy Bacon Breadcrumbs in the next step. You will use the rest in the soup itself. Remove all but about 3 table-spoons of rendered fat from the pot. Then use 3 tablespoons of this removed bacon fat for Crispy Bacon Breadcrumbs and use remaining fat for another purpose or dis-card. Turn off heat and set pot aside.

3 Prepare Crispy Bacon Breadcrumbs in separate skillet and set aside.

4 Reheat pot over medium-high heat. Then add anchovy and cook while stirring for about 1 minute or until it dissolves in fat. Add tomatoes, shallots, celery, green onions, and garlic. Cook for about 4 minutes, or until vegetables have softened a bit, stirring occasionally.

5 Sprinkle flour on top of vegetables. Stir to coat and continue stirring for 1 to 2 minutes while flour cooks. Gradually pour in wine and whisk mixture quickly to fully incorporate flour into liquid until smooth. Then stir to loosen and scrape up any browned bits on bottom of pot.

6 Add clam juice, potatoes (drain first if being held in water), bell peppers, hot sauce, dried herbs, and black pepper. Mix until all ingredients are well combined.

7 Cover pot and bring mixture to a simmer. Simmer, partially covered, until potatoes are tender, stirring frequently (about 15 to 20 minutes). Stir in clams, lemon juice, and remaining crispy bacon and cook just long enough to heat clams. Turn off heat and stir in parsley.

8 Ladle soup into bowls and top with Crispy Bacon Breadcrumbs.

recipe notes

• Be sure to save and strain the clam juice from the canned clams—it's an important part of the recipe.

• Canned clams are already fully cooked and just need to be heated. You should yield about 12 to 13 ounces strained clams from 6 (6.5-ounce) cans chopped clams.

crispy bacon breadcrumbs

3 tablespoons bacon fat or unsalted butter
½ cup finely diced red bell pepper (about ½ medium-sized pepper)
½ cup finely chopped green onion (about 2 onions)
¾ cup plain panko breadcrumbs
½ cup grated Pecorino Romano cheese
½ cup finely chopped crispy bacon pieces
⅓ cup chopped fresh flat-leaf parsley
1 tablespoon lemon zest
¼ teaspoon black pepper

Melt bacon fat or butter in small skillet over medium-low heat. Add bell peppers and chives and cook for 1 minute.

Add remaining breadcrumb ingredients, and mix until all ingredients are well combined. Cook, stirring continuously, until breadcrumbs are toasted (about 2 to 3 minutes). Remove from heat and set aside, uncovered, at room temperature.

You can make these breadcrumbs 3 to 4 hours in advance and hold them, uncovered, at room temperature.

shrimp pad thai soup | *Serves 6 to 8*

Years ago, early in my professional food career, I took a one-week class on Southeast Asian cooking. It was eye-opening and educational to learn about so many ingredients that I had never eaten, used, or even heard of. It was during this class, believe it or not, that I had my first pad Thai, a classic stir-fried rice noodle dish commonly served as street food in Thailand and in Thai restaurants all around the world. It usually contains any combination of chicken, shrimp, beef or tofu, peanuts, bean sprouts, a scrambled egg, and an assortment of vegetables. Its secret, though, is in its complex sauce, made with the unique and pungent flavors of uncommon ingredients including fish sauce, tamarind paste, and palm sugar. The result is a comforting noodle dish with an unmatched depth of flavor.

This SOUPified pad Thai is for the noodle soup lovers out there. Sticking with items that you can find in almost any supermarket's ethnic food aisle, this recipe is mostly about the ingredient prep, but it comes together rather quickly once you turn on the heat. It's reminiscent of a hearty, warming bowl of Asian noodle soup, with long silky rice noodles in a super-savory broth. Enjoy it the same way—with a large soup spoon and chopsticks (or a fork) to grab onto those long noodles!

ingredients

6 tablespoons smooth peanut butter

5 tablespoons low-sodium soy sauce

3 tablespoons fish sauce

3 tablespoons rice vinegar

3 tablespoons brown sugar

4 tablespoons high-heat oil, such as peanut, corn, safflower, or coconut oil

2 cups diced shallot (about 4 shallots)

1 heaping cup shredded carrot (about 4 ounces)

2 tablespoons grated fresh ginger or 1½ teaspoons ground ginger

1½ teaspoons crushed red pepper (optional)

9 cups low-sodium vegetable, seafood, or chicken broth

8 ounces rice or Pad Thai noodles, soaked for 20 to 30 minutes in enough water to cover

1 pound shrimp, peeled, deveined, tail off, cut into bite-sized pieces

2 cups bite-sized vegetables (optional, see recipe note, page 33)

1 cup chopped green onion (about 4 onions)

6 tablespoons fresh lime juice (zest limes first)

4 tablespoons chopped cilantro, leaves only

1 tablespoon lime zest

2 cups bean sprouts, rinsed and drained (for topping)

¾ cup chopped roasted peanuts (for topping)

instructions

1 Soak rice noodles. Mix the following ingredients together in a small bowl until well blended, then set aside: peanut butter, soy sauce, fish sauce, rice vinegar, and brown sugar.

2 Heat oil in 6-quart (or larger) pot or Dutch oven over medium heat. Add shallots, carrots, ginger, and crushed red pepper. Cook for about 6 minutes, or until carrots have softened a bit, stirring occasionally to prevent burning.

3 Add 2 cups broth and stir to loosen and scrape up any browned bits on bottom of pot.

4 Add remaining broth and peanut butter mixture, and mix well. Cover pot and bring mixture to a boil. Drain and rinse rice noodles, then add them to boiling broth, and mix well.

5 Cook noodles, uncovered, for 5 minutes while stirring frequently so that they do not stick or get clumpy. Then, reduce heat to low and stir in shrimp, vegetables (if including), green onions, lime juice, cilantro, and lime zest.

6 Lightly simmer, uncovered, for 5 more minutes, stirring regularly, then turn off heat.

7 Ladle soup into bowls and top with bean sprouts and peanuts.

recipe notes

- Soaking the rice noodles is key! It removes much of their unwanted starch and keeps the soup from becoming too thick.

- Here are some great options if you choose to add additional vegetables to this soup: red bell pepper, bok choy, baby spinach, mushrooms, and broccoli florets.

- If you're unable to find bean sprouts, just omit them or consider these crunchy alternatives: napa cabbage, snow peas, or zucchini noodles.

- You can definitely use the thinner vermicelli rice noodles and no soaking is required!

- Be sure to zest the limes before squeezing out their juice.

- Not a fan of shrimp? No problem—both chicken and tofu are great substitutions.

Chicken Tikka Masala Soup, page 54

chicken *soups*

chicken marsala soup | *Serves 4 to 6*

We all need a little chicken Marsala in our lives from time to time. A staple of every Italian American red sauce restaurant across America, it's a delightful combination of golden, seared chicken breasts and earthy mushrooms, cooked in a rich pan sauce of sweet, fortified Marsala wine and good ol' full-fat butter. It is creamy and savory and comforting and decadent all at once.

This Chicken Marsala Soup recipe was one of the first I developed for this book. As a long-time eater and cooker of Marsala everything, I knew the flavors would translate perfectly to soup form, and I was thrilled to have that confirmed upon my first spoonful. I may just permanently embrace the bowl on this one.

ingredients

1 pound boneless, skinless chicken breasts
Pinch salt and black pepper
¾ cup all-purpose flour, divided
7 tablespoons unsalted butter, divided
2 cups diced shallots (about 4 shallots)
1 cup diced celery (about 3 to 4 ribs)
1½ cups dry Marsala wine
4 cups low-sodium chicken broth

1 pound white mushrooms, coarsely chopped
½ cup chopped sun-dried tomatoes, drained of any oil
½ teaspoon salt
¼ teaspoon black pepper
¼ cup heavy cream

instructions

1 Brown chicken: Pat chicken breasts dry with paper towel, then sprinkle both sides with salt and pepper. Dredge breasts completely in ½ cup flour, then shake off excess. Set aside on plate. Melt 4 tablespoons butter in 6-quart (or larger) pot or Dutch oven over medium-high heat. When butter has melted, transfer chicken breasts to pot and sear them until browned on both sides (about 3 to 4 minutesper side). The chicken does not need to be fully cooked at this point. Transfer seared breasts to cutting board and let them rest for 3 minutes. Then cut them into bite-sized pieces (about ¾-inch dice). Set aside.

2 Reduce heat to medium, then add remaining 3 tablespoons butter to pot. Add shallots and celery and cook for about 4

minutes, or until vegetables have softened a bit, stirring occasionally.

3 Sprinkle remaining ¼ cup flour on top of shallot mixture; stir to coat and continue stirring for 1 to 2 minutes while flour cooks. Gradually pour in wine and whisk mixture quickly to fully incorporate flour into liquid until smooth. Then stir to loosen and scrape up any browned bits on bottom of pot.

4 Add broth, mushrooms, sun-dried tomatoes, salt, black pepper, and reserved chicken. Mix until all ingredients are well combined. Cover pot and bring mixture to a simmer, stirring occasionally. Simmer, partially covered, until celery is soft and chicken is fully cooked (about 15 minutes).

5 Reduce heat to low. Then whisk in cream and cook for another 3 minutes while stirring. Turn off heat.

6 Ladle soup into bowls.

recipe notes

- **TIME SAVERS TIP:** If you're short on time, you can adapt this recipe by skipping the raw chicken and adding 1 pound chopped roasted or rotisserie chicken to the soup at the same time as the mushrooms.

- For something extra hearty, consider folding in some cooked egg noodles right before serving.

chicken piccata soup | *Serves 4 to 6*

"You had me at fried capers." *This is what a friend said to me when I first told her about my vision for this soup. Chicken piccata in its normal form is pretty darned magical—a simple dish of seared chicken breasts finished in a luxurious buttery, lemon-caper sauce. Once SOUPified, the flavors get transported to a whole other level.*

While chicken soup in almost any form is the comforting food we all crave when needing a culinary hug, this Chicken Piccata Soup might be considered its smarter, more attractive cousin. It blends richness, juiciness, and tartness all into one mouthwatering spoonful. And that Fried Caper topping? It is, indeed, magical.

ingredients

1½ pounds boneless, skinless chicken breasts

Pinch salt and black pepper

¾ cup all-purpose flour, divided

7 tablespoons unsalted butter, divided

2 cups diced shallots (about 4 shallots)

1 cup diced celery (about 3 to 4 ribs)

¼ cup chopped garlic (9 to 10 cloves)

2 cups dry white wine, such as pinot grigio

5 cups low-sodium chicken broth

½ teaspoon salt

¼ teaspoon black pepper

¼ cup white miso

6 tablespoons heavy cream

4 packed cups chopped fresh baby spinach (about 6 ounces)

½ cup fresh lemon juice (zest lemons first)

1 tablespoon lemon zest

1 recipe Fried Capers (page 41)

instructions

1 Prepare Fried Capers and set aside.

2 Brown chicken: Pat chicken breasts dry with paper towel, then sprinkle both sides with salt and pepper. Dredge breasts completely in ½ cup flour, then shake off excess. Set aside on plate. Melt 4 tablespoons butter in 6-quart (or larger) pot or Dutch oven over medium-high heat. When butter has melt-ed, transfer chicken breasts to pot and sear them until browned on both sides (about 3 to 4 minutes per side). The chicken does not need to be fully cooked at this point. Transfer seared breasts to cutting board and let them rest for 3 minutes. Then cut them into bite-sized pieces (about ¾-inch dice). Set aside.

3 Reduce heat to medium, then add remaining 3 tablespoons butter to pot. Add shallots, celery, and garlic. Cook for about 4 minutes,

or until the vegetables have softened a bit, stirring occasionally.

4 Sprinkle remaining ¼ cup flour on top of shallot mixture. Stir to coat and continue stirring for 1 to 2 minutes while flour cooks. Gradually pour in wine and whisk mixture quickly to fully incorporate flour into liquid until smooth. Then stir to loosen and scrape up any browned bits on bottom of pot.

5 Add broth, salt, black pepper, and reserved chicken. Mix until all ingredients are well combined. Cover pot and bring mixture to a simmer, stirring occasionally. Simmer, partially covered, until celery is soft and chicken is fully cooked (about 15 minutes).

6 Reduce heat to medium-low, then whisk in miso and cream until well incorporated. Simmer for 2 minutes. Then stir in spinach, lemon juice, and lemon zest and turn off heat.

7 Ladle soup into bowls and top with Fried Capers.

recipe notes

- **TIME SAVERS TIP:** If you're short on time, you can adapt this recipe by skipping the raw chicken and adding 1½ pounds chopped roasted or rotisserie chicken to the soup right before the cream.

- If you are unable to find miso, you can use 2 tablespoons low-sodium soy sauce.

- Be sure to zest the lemons before squeezing out their juice!

fried capers

3 tablespoons unsalted butter
½ cup capers, drained if in brine

Make sure that capers are completely dry by placing them on paper towels and patting them dry.

Melt butter in small skillet over medium heat. When butter has melted, add capers and fry them in butter for about 4 minutes or until they get crispy, stirring occasionally. Transfer them to a paper towel to drain and set aside, uncovered, at room temperature.

You can make these capers 3 to 4 hours in advance and hold them, uncovered, at room temperature.

chicken cacciatore soup | *Serves 6 to 8*

Chicken cacciatore is one of those recipes that seems to have dozens, if not hundreds, of versions. This traditional Italian dish is, at its core, a slow-cooked combination of moist dark chicken meat, dry wine, and a savory tomato sauce. Its flavors are deep, bold, and earthy and its spirit is rustic, like the hunters it celebrates. Cacciatore means "hunter" in Italian.

SOUPified Chicken Cacciatore is similarly rustic, containing tender pieces of chicken thigh, aromatic onions, mushrooms, bell peppers, earthy red wine, rosemary, and lots of bright tomato flavor to bring it all together. The dish's characteristic boldness shines through in this brothy bowl version. It comes together pretty quickly, making it a perfect weeknight meal.

ingredients

1½ pounds boneless, skinless chicken thighs, excess fat removed

Pinch salt and black pepper

½ cup all-purpose flour

6 tablespoons olive oil, divided

2 cups diced yellow onion (about 1 medium onion)

1 cup diced celery (about 3 to 4 ribs)

¼ cup chopped garlic (9 to 10 cloves)

¼ teaspoon crushed red pepper

3 tablespoons tomato paste

2 cups dry red wine, such as merlot

4 cups low-sodium chicken broth

1 can (14.5 ounces) diced tomatoes

1 fresh rosemary sprig

1 teaspoon finely chopped fresh rosemary

1 teaspoon dried basil

1 teaspoon dried oregano

½ teaspoon salt

¼ teaspoon black pepper

1 pound coarsely chopped mushrooms

2 cups diced bell peppers (about 2 medium-sized peppers)

3 packed cups chopped fresh baby spinach (about 4 ounces)

instructions

1 Brown chicken: Pat chicken thighs dry with paper towel, then sprinkle both sides with salt and pepper. Dredge thighs completely in flour, then shake off excess. Set aside on plate. Heat 4 tablespoons oil in 6-quart (or larger) pot or Dutch oven over medium-high heat. Transfer chicken thighs to pot and sear them until browned on both sides (about 3 to 4 minutes per side). The chicken does not need to be fully cooked at this point. Transfer seared thighs to cutting board and let them rest for 3 minutes. Then cut them into bite-sized pieces (about ¾-inch dice). Set aside.

2 Reduce heat to medium, then add remaining 2 tablespoons oil to pot. Add onions, celery, garlic, and crushed red pepper. Cook for about 4 minutes, or until vegetables have softened a bit, stirring occasionally.

3 Move onion mixture to one side of pot. Add tomato paste and cook it for about 30 seconds. Add wine and stir to loosen and scrape up any browned bits on bottom of pot.

4 Add broth, tomatoes, rosemary, dried herbs, salt, black pepper, and reserved chicken. Mix until all ingredients are well combined. Cover pot and bring mixture to a simmer, stirring occasionally.

5 Add mushrooms and peppers and stir until well combined. Continue simmering, uncovered, until peppers are tender and chicken is fully cooked (about 10 to 15 minutes).

6 Remove and discard rosemary sprig. Fold in spinach and turn off heat.

7 Ladle soup into bowls.

recipe notes

- **TIME SAVERS TIP:** If you're short on time, you can adapt this recipe by skipping the raw chicken and adding 1½ pounds chopped roasted or rotisserie chicken to the soup at the same time as the mushrooms.

- For something extra hearty, consider folding in some cooked egg noodles right before serving.

chicken cordon bleu soup | *Serves 6 to 8*

I will always remember my first chicken Cordon Bleu. It was way back in college on the Sunday night after Thanksgiving, when we all returned to the dorms after the long holiday weekend. My roommate, Liz, brought back a foil tray of it from her mom who made it just "for the girls." Chicken Cordon Bleu was one of her specialties we had all heard about for months. That first bite of chicken rolled with salty ham and earthy Swiss cheese paired with a buttery sauce was magical. It's a classic pairing that unapologetically lacks significant innovation from one recipe to the next because there's no need for it. Why mess with perfection?

This one's for you, Betty.

ingredients

8 tablespoons unsalted butter, divided

12 ounces ham steak or leftover baked ham cut into ½-inch dice

1 pound boneless, skinless chicken breasts

Pinch salt and black pepper

¾ cup all-purpose flour, divided

2 cups diced shallot (about 4 shallots)

1 cup diced celery (about 3 to 4 ribs)

¼ cup chopped garlic (9 to 10 cloves)

2 cups dry white wine, such as pinot grigio

2½ cups low-sodium chicken broth

2½ cups whole milk

1 tablespoon Dijon-style mustard

1 teaspoon dried thyme

½ teaspoon salt

¼ teaspoon black pepper

1 pound Swiss cheese, grated or cut into very small pieces

4 packed cups chopped fresh baby spinach (about 6 ounces)

1 recipe Porky Breadcrumbs (page 47)

instructions

1 Prepare Porky Breadcrumbs and set aside.

2 Brown ham: Melt 5 tablespoons butter in 6-quart (or larger) pot or Dutch oven over medium-high heat. When butter has melted, add ham and cook until it starts to crisp and brown a bit, about 8 to 10 minutes, stirring occasionally. Remove ham with a slotted spoon and set it aside to drain on paper towels. Reduce heat to low while preparing chicken.

3 Brown chicken: Pat chicken breasts dry with paper towel, then sprinkle both sides with salt and pepper. Dredge breasts completely in ½ cup flour, then shake off excess and set aside on plate. Return pot to medium-high heat. Transfer chicken breasts to pot and sear them until browned on both sides (about 3 to 4 minutes per side). The chicken does not

need to be fully cooked at this point. Transfer seared breasts to cutting board and let them rest for 3 minutes. Then cut them into bite-sized pieces (about ¾-inch dice). Set aside.

4 Reduce heat to medium. Add remaining 3 tablespoons butter to pot. Add shallots, celery, and garlic and cook for about 4 minutes, or until vegetables have softened a bit, stirring occasionally.

5 Sprinkle remaining ¼ cup flour on top of shallot mixture. Stir to coat and continue stirring for 1 to 2 minutes while flour cooks. Gradually pour in wine and whisk mixture quickly to fully incorporate flour into liquid until smooth. Then, stir to loosen and scrape up any browned bits on bottom of pot.

6 Add broth, milk, mustard, thyme, salt, black pepper, reserved ham, and chicken. Stir until all ingredients are well combined. Cover pot and bring mixture to a simmer, stirring occasionally. Continue simmering, partially covered, about 10 to 15 minutes, until all vegetables are soft and chicken is fully cooked. Do not boil soup once milk is added to prevent curdling.

7 Turn heat to low. Gradually stir in cheese, 1 cup at a time, ensuring each cup has melted before adding the next. Fold in spinach and turn off heat.

8 Ladle soup into bowls and top with Porky Breadcrumbs.

recipe note

• **TIME SAVERS TIP:** If you're short on time, you can adapt this recipe by skipping the raw chicken and adding 1 pound chopped roasted or rotisserie chicken to the soup right before the cheese.

porky breadcrumbs

3 tablespoons unsalted butter
½ cup finely chopped ham (about 3 ounces)
1 cup plain breadcrumbs
¼ cup Pecorino Romano cheese
¼ teaspoon black pepper

Melt butter in small skillet over medium heat. Add ham and cook for 5 to 6 minutes, or until it starts to brown.

Reduce heat to medium-low. Stir in breadcrumbs, cheese, and black pepper. Cook until breadcrumbs are toasted, about 2 to 3 minutes, stirring continuously. Remove from heat and set aside, uncovered, at room temperature.

You can make these breadcrumbs 3 to 4 hours in advance and hold them, uncovered, at room temperature.

chicken burrito soup | *Serves 6 to 8*

While I love the flavors and textures of a classic chicken burrito, I have to admit that I actually don't love eating them. There's something about its packaged format that just doesn't resonate with me. Strange, I know, especially since I adore sandwiches and almost all foods placed in a roll or between two slices of bread.

Maybe it was my desire to find a burrito format that I enjoyed, or maybe it was just that I thought chicken, beans, rice, tomato, peppers, and lime would make a darn delicious soup. Either way, this SOUPified Chicken Burrito is not to be missed. It's like a supreme burrito in a bowl, with tons of personality and just enough creaminess to make you reconsider your next trip to the build-your-own-burrito bar.

ingredients

1½ pounds boneless, skinless chicken breasts

Pinch salt and black pepper

¾ cup all-purpose flour, divided

6 tablespoons olive oil, divided

2 cups diced yellow onion (about 1 medium onion)

1 cup chopped green onion (about 4 onions)

½ cup diced jalapeño peppers, seeds and stem removed (about 2 peppers)

¼ cup chopped garlic (9 to 10 cloves)

6 cups low-sodium chicken broth

2 cans (15 ounces) cooked black beans, drained and rinsed

1 can (14.5 ounces) diced fire-roasted or plain tomatoes

½ cup white rice (3½ ounces)

1½ teaspoons salt

1 teaspoon dried Mexican or regular oregano

½ teaspoon chipotle chili powder

½ teaspoon paprika

¼ teaspoon black pepper

¼ teaspoon cumin powder

2 cups diced bell pepper (about 2 medium-sized peppers)

4 ounces cream cheese, softened, broken into small pieces

⅓ cup chopped fresh cilantro, leaves only

¼ cup fresh lime juice (zest limes first)

1 tablespoon lime zest

1 cup shredded cheddar cheese (optional topping)

1 cup sour cream (optional topping)

Tortilla chips, for serving (optional)

instructions

1 Brown chicken: Pat chicken breasts dry with paper towel, then sprinkle both sides with salt and pepper. Dredge breasts completely in ½ cup flour, then shake off excess. Set aside on plate. Heat 4 tablespoons oil in 6-quart (or larger) pot or Dutch oven over medium-high heat. Transfer chicken breasts to pot and sear them until browned on both sides (about 3 to 4 minutes per side). The chicken does not need to be fully cooked at this point. Transfer seared breasts to cutting board and let them rest for 3 minutes. Then cut them into bite-sized pieces (about ¾-inch dice). Set aside.

2 Reduce heat to medium, then add remaining 2 tablespoons oil to pot. Add onions, jalapeño, and garlic. Cook for about 4 minutes or until onions have softened a bit, stirring occasionally.

3 Sprinkle remaining ¼ cup flour on top of onion mixture; stir to coat and continue stirring for 1 to 2 minutes while flour cooks. Gradually pour in 2 cups broth and whisk mixture quickly to fully incorporate flour into liquid until smooth. Then stir to loosen and scrape up any browned bits on bottom of pot.

4 Add remaining broth, beans, tomatoes, rice, spices, dried herbs, and reserved chicken. Mix until all ingredients are well combined. Partially cover pot and bring mixture to a simmer, stirring often so that rice does not stick. Depending on the variety of rice that you use, it may take from 12 to 20 minutes until rice is mostly cooked.

5 Once rice is mostly cooked, stir in bell peppers. Simmer for another 8 to 10 minutes or until peppers have softened.

6 Reduce heat to low. Gradually add cream cheese and stir until it has completely melted and dissolved in soup. Mix in cilantro, lime juice, and lime zest and turn off heat.

7 Ladle soup into bowls, top with optional toppings, and serve with tortilla chips, if desired.

recipe notes

- **TIME SAVERS TIP:** If you're short on time, you can adapt this recipe by skipping the raw chicken and adding 1½ pounds chopped roasted or rotisserie chicken to the soup at the same time as the bell peppers.

- Chicken breasts or thighs work equally well in this recipe—use whichever you prefer.

- Include some or all of the jalapeño seeds if you prefer a soup with lots of heat!

- If you are unable to find chipotle powder, substitute smoked paprika.

- Be sure to zest the limes before squeezing out their juice.

chicken scarpariello soup | *Serves 6 to 8*

Chicken scarpariello, also known as "Shoemaker's Chicken," is a classic Italian American dish that is hearty in a stick-to-your-ribs sort of way. It's full of rich Italian sausage, juicy chicken thighs, potatoes, bell peppers, and onions, with a defining vinegary, sweet-and-sour flavor from its signature ingredient: hot and pungent vinegar peppers.

This SOUPified version remains close to its core recipe, containing a tangy zestiness from dry white wine, red wine vinegar, and a respectable amount of both hot cherry peppers in vinegar and their sweet and spicy brine. It even has the crunch normally achieved by roasting through the crispy Tiny Fried Potato topping. It's a celebration of flavors and textures with a sublime aroma. Enjoy it at your next get-together with a bottle of your favorite red wine and loaf of rustic Italian bread.

ingredients

12 ounces boneless, skinless chicken thighs, excess fat removed

Pinch salt and black pepper

½ cup all-purpose flour

4 tablespoons olive oil

12 ounces hot or sweet Italian sausage, casings removed

2 cups diced yellow onions (about 1 medium onion)

½ cup chopped garlic (18 to 20 cloves)

½ cup chopped fresh sage

1 tablespoon tomato paste

2 cups dry white wine, such as pinot grigio

¼ cup red wine vinegar

5 cups low-sodium chicken broth

1 russet potato cut into ¼-inch pieces, held in cold water to prevent browning

½ cup chopped hot cherry peppers in vinegar, drained

2 tablespoons vinegar brine from hot cherry peppers

1 teaspoon dried oregano

½ teaspoon salt

¼ teaspoon black pepper

2 cups diced red bell peppers (about 2 medium-sized peppers)

¼ cup chopped fresh flat-leaf parsley

1 recipe Tiny Fried Potatoes (page 53)

instructions

1 Prepare Tiny Fried Potatoes and set aside.

2 Brown chicken: Pat chicken thighs dry with paper towel, then sprinkle both sides with salt and pepper. Dredge thighs completely in flour, then shake off excess and set aside on plate. Heat oil in 6-quart (or larger) pot or Dutch oven over medium-high heat. Transfer chicken thighs to pot and sear them until browned on both sides (about 3 to 4 minutes per side). The chicken does not need to be fully cooked at this point. Transfer seared thighs to cutting board and let them rest for 3 minutes. Then cut them into bite-sized pieces (about ¾-inch dice). Set aside.

3 Add sausage to pot. Cook for about 6 to 8 minutes, or until it has browned. Break up sausage into bite-sized pieces while stirring.

4 Reduce heat to medium. Add onions, garlic, and sage. Cook for about 4 minutes, or until vegetables have softened a bit, stirring occasionally.

5 Move onion mixture to one side of pot. Add tomato paste and cook it for about 30 seconds. Add wine and vinegar and stir to loosen and scrape up any browned bits on bottom of pot.

6 Add broth, potatoes (drain first if being held in water), cherry peppers, vinegar brine, dried oregano, salt, black pepper, and reserved chicken. Mix until all ingredients are well combined. Cover pot and bring mixture to a simmer, stirring occasionally. Simmer, partially covered, for about 15 to 20 minutes or until potatoes are mostly cooked. Then stir in bell peppers. Continue simmering, partially covered, until potatoes and peppers are tender and chicken is fully cooked (about 6 to 8 minutes).

7 Turn off heat and mix in parsley.

8 Ladle soup into bowls and top with Tiny Fried Potatoes.

recipe note

- **TIME SAVERS TIP:** If you're short on time, you can adapt this recipe by skipping the raw chicken and adding 12 ounces chopped roasted or rotisserie chicken to the soup at the same time as the bell peppers.

tiny fried potatoes

¼ to ½ cup olive oil or as needed
2 russet potatoes cut into ½-inch dice
Pinch salt

Heat oil in large skillet over medium heat. Once oil starts to spread out and glisten, add diced potatoes and spread them out into single layer in pan. Fry them until crispy. Do this in batches, if necessary, and stir potatoes a couple times while frying to brown them on multiple sides. This will take about 12 to 15 minutes.

When brown and crispy, remove potatoes with slotted spoon and transfer them to paper towels to drain. Sprinkle them with salt immediately. Set aside, uncovered, at room temperature.

You can also make these potatoes in your oven: Toss potatoes with oil. Arrange potatoes in single layer on parchment-lined sheet pan. Roast on middle rack at 400°F for about 30 to 45 minutes, or until brown and crispy. Remove from oven and sprinkle with salt immediately.

chicken tikka masala soup | *Serves 6 to 8*

While a staple on almost every Indian restaurant's menu in both the United States and Great Britain, chicken tikka masala is actually a British invention and not a dish native to India. It's a satisfying combination of tender chicken in a creamy tomato-based sauce that has been infused with a slew of fragrant spices and lots of deeply caramelized onions. It gets its signature flavor from earthy garam masala, a spice blend known for its warming qualities.

And that is just how I would describe this soup—warm. It's warm in spirit. Warm in a "close your eyes and breathe deeply" sort of way. Warm as in friendly, and warm as in comfortable. It's like a good friend inviting you over to have a bite. Accept and enjoy.

ingredients

1½ pounds boneless, skinless chicken breasts

Pinch salt, black pepper, and garam masala

½ cup all-purpose flour

4 tablespoons unsalted butter or ghee (see Recipe Note, page 56)

4 cups diced yellow onions (about 1 large onion)

¼ cup diced jalapeño peppers, seeds and stem removed (about 1 pepper)

¼ cup chopped garlic (9 to 10 cloves)

2 tablespoons grated fresh ginger or 1½ teaspoon ground ginger

1 tablespoon garam masala

1 teaspoon curry powder

1 teaspoon turmeric

¼ teaspoon cayenne pepper

½ cup tomato paste

6 cups low-sodium chicken broth

1 can (28 ounces) whole, diced, or crushed tomatoes

1 can (14 ounces) coconut milk

1 cup roasted red pepper, drained, no seeds (about 8 ounces)

1 teaspoon salt

¼ teaspoon black pepper

½ cup basmati rice (3½ ounces)

½ cup heavy cream

¼ cup fresh lime juice (zest limes first)

1 tablespoon lime zest

1 cup chopped fresh cilantro

instructions

1 Brown chicken: Pat chicken breasts dry with paper towel. Then sprinkle both sides with salt, pepper, and garam masala. Dredge breasts completely in flour, then shake off excess. Set aside on plate. Melt butter or ghee in 6-quart (or larger) pot or Dutch oven over medium-high heat. When butter has melted, transfer chicken breasts to pot and sear them until browned on both sides (about 3 to 4 minutes per side). The chicken does not need to be fully cooked at this point. Transfer seared breasts to cutting board and let them rest for 3 minutes. Then cut them into bite-sized pieces (about ¾-inch dice). Set aside.

2 Caramelize onions: Reduce heat to medium, then add onions and slowly cook until brown and caramelized, stirring regularly. This may take 20 to 25 minutes. If onions start to burn, reduce heat, add ½ cup water or stock, and scrape bottom of pot with spatula.

3 Once onions have caramelized, add jalapeño, garlic, ginger, garam masala, curry powder, turmeric, and cayenne. Cook for another 2 to 3 minutes, or until spices are fragrant, stirring occasionally.

4 Move onion mixture to one side of pot. Then add tomato paste and cook it for about 30 seconds. Add 2 cups broth and stir to loosen and scrape up any browned bits on bottom of pot.

5 Add remaining broth, tomatoes, coconut milk, roasted peppers, salt, and black pepper. Stir until all ingredients are well combined. Cover pot and bring mixture to a simmer, stirring occasionally. Simmer, partially covered, for about 8 to 10 minutes, or until all vegetables have softened. Reduce heat to low. Carefully purée mixture until smooth using an immersion blender.

6 Increase heat to medium. Add rice and reserved chicken and stir until all ingredients are well combined. Bring mixture back to a simmer and cook, uncovered, until rice is tender, stirring frequently so that rice does not stick. Depending on the variety of rice that you use, it may take anywhere from 12 to 20 minutes until rice is tender.

7 Once rice is cooked, reduce heat to low. Then whisk in cream and cook for another 2 minutes while stirring. Stir in lime juice, lime zest, and cilantro, then turn off heat.

8 Ladle soup into bowls.

recipe notes

- Ghee is a nutty, caramelized version of clarified butter that is traditional in Indian cuisine. If you have some on hand, definitely use it in this recipe. Otherwise, unsalted butter works perfectly well.

- Chicken breasts or thighs work equally well in this recipe—use whichever you prefer!

- Don't skip or rush through the onion caramelization step. The sweet, dramatic flavor that results from slowly cooking the onions is key to the overall flavor in this soup.

- Include some or all of the jalapeño seeds if you prefer a soup with lots of heat!

- Be sure to zest the limes before squeezing out their juice.

Chicken Cordon Bleu Soup, page 45

Lasagne Soup, page 63

beef *soups*

bacon cheeseburger soup | *Serves 4 to 6*

This soup doesn't need much of an introduction. It is, in fact, the SOUPified version of one of the most popular comfort foods in America, the beloved bacon cheeseburger. Hearty, rich, and satisfying like its non-bowl counterpart, this Bacon Cheeseburger Soup might just be the ultimate comfort food soup out there. It's a creamy blend of ground beef, crispy bacon, savory veggies, just the right amount of seasonings, and copious amounts of sharp cheddar cheese all made in one pot! Once you top off the whole thing with crunchy Hamburger Roll Croutons, sesame seeds, and even more crispy bacon, you will swear you're in cheeseburger heaven.

There is so much flavor in this soup that it is guaranteed to be a hit with the whole family, even the picky eaters and those with hearty appetites! If you are looking to amp up your cheeseburger game, I highly recommend trying this fun and delicious SOUPified Bacon Cheeseburger.

ingredients

1 pound bacon cut into ½-inch strips while raw

1½ pounds lean ground beef (90/10 is perfect)

2 cups diced yellow onions (about 1 medium onion)

1 heaping cup shredded carrots (about 4 ounces)

1 cup diced celery (about 3 to 4 ribs)

¼ cup all-purpose flour

2½ cups low-sodium beef broth

2½ cups whole milk

12 ounces russet potatoes, peeled and diced, held in cold water to prevent browning

6 tablespoons pickle juice (from your favorite pickle jar)

1 tablespoon Dijon-style mustard

1 tablespoon Worcestershire sauce

2 teaspoons hot sauce

1 teaspoon salt

½ teaspoon black pepper

1 pound sharp cheddar cheese, shredded or cut into very small pieces

1 cup chopped green onion (about 4 onions)

¼ cup white sesame seeds (optional topping)

1 cup sour cream (optional topping)

1 recipe Hamburger Roll Croutons (page 62)

instructions

1 Prepare Hamburger Roll Croutons and set aside.

2 Cook bacon: Place bacon in 6-quart (or larger) pot or Dutch over medium heat. Slowly cook it until it becomes crispy and most of the fat has been rendered. Remove bacon with slotted spoon and set it aside to drain on paper towels. Remove all but about 2 tablespoons of rendered fat from the pot and use for other purpose or discard. Leave enough fat to cover bottom of pot.

3 Brown beef: Increase heat to medium-high. Then add beef, onions, carrots, and celery and cook for about 6 to 8 minutes, or until all the beef has browned. Break it up into bite-sized pieces while stirring.

4 Sprinkle flour on top of beef mixture; stir to coat and continue stirring for 1 to 2 minutes while flour cooks. Gradually pour in broth

and whisk mixture quickly to fully incorporate flour into liquid until smooth. Then stir to loosen and scrape up any browned bits on bottom of pot.

5 Add milk, potatoes (drain first if being held in water), pickle juice, mustard, Worcestershire and hot sauces, salt, and black pepper and stir until all ingredients are well combined. Cover pot and bring mixture to a simmer. Simmer, partially covered, about 12 to 15 minutes, until potatoes are tender, stirring frequently. Do not boil soup once milk is added to prevent curdling.

6 Reduce heat to low. Then gradually whisk in cheeses, 1 cup at a time, ensuring each cup has melted before adding the next. Stir in green onions and about ¾ of the crispy bacon, then turn off heat.

7 Ladle soup into bowls and top with Hamburger Roll Croutons, remaining bacon, and optional toppings, if desired.

recipe note

- If you prefer a different cheese, here are some great alternatives to cheddar: Monterey Jack, American, Gruyère, and Swiss.

hamburger roll croutons

3 hamburger rolls cut into ½-inch cubes
2 to 3 tablespoons olive oil
Pinch salt and black pepper

Arrange rack in middle of the oven, then preheat to 375°F.

Toss cubed bread with oil. Then arrange cubes in a single layer on parchment-lined sheet pan and sprinkle with salt and pepper.

Bake bread on middle rack for about 8 to 10 minutes or until golden and crispy. Set aside, uncovered, at room temperature.

You can make these croutons 3 to 4 hours in advance and hold them, uncovered, at room temperature.

lasagne soup | *Serves 6 to 8*

I wouldn't be a good Italian American if I did not SOUPify this quintessential family classic. Lasagne is beloved for a reason—its layers of savory beef, creamy cheeses, tomato sauce, fresh herbs, and silky noodles offer flavor and richness unmatched in most other dishes. Eating it is like a big hug from Mom. And Grandmom. And who doesn't love a big hug?

Do I dare say that you might even consider ditching the somewhat laborious, traditional version of lasagne for this more streamlined, SOUPified pot of deliciousness? I do. Indeed. All the flavors and textures of mouthwatering lasagne in comforting soup form—it's an easy decision, if you ask me!

ingredients

3 tablespoons olive oil, divided

1 pound lean ground beef (90/10 is perfect)

2 cups diced yellow onion (about
1 medium onion)

1 cup lightly packed, chopped fresh basil
leaves, divided

¼ cup chopped garlic (9 to 10 cloves)

2 teaspoons salt

1 teaspoon black pepper

½ teaspoon crushed red pepper

½ cup tomato paste

6 cups low-sodium beef or chicken broth

1 can (28 ounces) whole tomatoes crushed
into small pieces by hand

2 teaspoons dried basil

1½ teaspoons dried oregano

8 lasagne sheets, broken into 1–2" random
pieces (9 ounces)

½ cup heavy cream

3½ packed cups chopped fresh baby
spinach (about 5 ounces)

1 recipe Cheese Topping (page 65)

instructions

1 Prepare Cheese Topping and set aside.

2 Brown beef: Heat 2 tablespoons oil in 6-quart
(or larger) pot or Dutch oven over medium-
high heat. Add beef, onions, ½ cup basil, garlic,
and spices. Cook for about 6 to 8 minutes, or
until all the beef has browned. Break it up into
bite-sized pieces while stirring.

3 Move beef mixture to one side of pot. Then
add tomato paste and cook it for about 30
seconds. Add 2 cups broth and stir to loos-
en and scrape up any browned bits on bottom of pot.

4 Add remaining broth, tomatoes, and dried
herbs and stir until all ingredients are well
combined. Cover pot and bring mixture to

a simmer, stirring occasionally. Simmer, partially covered, for about 6 to 8 minutes, or until vegetables have mostly softened. Add pasta and remaining 1 tablespoon oil and stir well.

5 Simmer, uncovered, until pasta is *al dente*, using instructions on pasta package as a guideline, stirring continuously so that pasta doesn't stick or get clumpy. Taste pasta along the way to monitor its doneness.

6 Once pasta is *al dente*, reduce heat to low. Then whisk in cream and spinach and cook for another 2 minutes while stirring. Add additional liquid if you want a brothier soup. Stir in remaining ½ cup basil, then turn off heat.

7 Ladle soup into bowls and top with a generous scoop of Cheese Topping. The cheese will melt once you stir it into the hot soup.

recipe notes

- If you prefer a more spoon-friendly pasta, try egg noodles, *campanelle* (flower-shaped pasta), or broken *Mafalda* (wide ribbons)— all work great and maintain the spirit of lasagne noodles!

- Drizzle the soup with some of your favorite extra-virgin olive oil for an extra-special indulgence.

- Italian pork sausage (out of its casing) and ground turkey are both great alternatives for the ground beef.

- If you're reheating this soup in the microwave, it's a great idea to place a spoonful of the cheese topping right in the bowl as it will melt nicely once heated.

cheese topping

1 cup whole milk ricotta cheese
1 cup shredded mozzarella cheese (about 4 ounces)
⅓ cup grated Pecorino Romano cheese
⅛ teaspoon black pepper

Mix all topping ingredients together until well combined.

You can make this 2 to 3 days in advance and hold it in the refrigerator. Bring this mixture to room temperature about 30 minutes before serving the soup.

philly cheesesteak soup | *Serves 6 to 8*

Having grown up in a suburb of the City of Brotherly Love, where cheesesteaks reign supreme, it makes sense that I would want to SOUPify this iconic regional favorite. I mean—I really, really love and often crave that classic combination of tender meat and gooey cheese stuffed into a soft sub roll. It's a bit of a guilty pleasure of mine that I don't indulge in frequently. For some reason, though, I feel it is much more acceptable to enjoy its SOUPified version on a more regular basis.

This Philly Cheesesteak Soup has all the flavors and textures as the original sandwich—as I love to order it myself—accented with copious amounts of fried onions, mushrooms, and hot pickled peppers, with provolone and American as my cheeses of choice, and with crunchy Sub Roll Croutons to mimic the signature roll. Feel free to make this soup your own by omitting the mushrooms, switching up the cheeses (Whiz, anyone?) or leaving the whole mixture chunky and not puréed. However you decide to order your rich and hearty Philly Cheesesteak Soup, it will surely be something that you will want to return to again and again.

ingredients

2 tablespoons olive oil

2 pounds ribeye steak, beef round sirloin, or top sirloin, cut into small, bite-sized pieces

6 tablespoons all-purpose flour, divided

1½ teaspoons salt, divided

1½ teaspoons black pepper, divided

1 teaspoon granulated garlic or garlic powder

4 tablespoons unsalted butter

3 cups diced yellow onion (about 1½ medium onions)

1 cup diced celery (about 3 to 4 ribs)

¼ cup chopped garlic (9 to 10 cloves)

1 cup dry white wine, such as pinot grigio

5 cups low-sodium beef or mushroom broth

1 pound chopped white mushrooms

4 teaspoons Worcestershire sauce

1 tablespoon hot sauce

10 ounces American cheese, shredded or cut into very small pieces

8 ounces sharp provolone cheese, shredded or cut into very small pieces

1 cup thinly sliced pickled banana peppers or pepperoncini peppers, drained (optional topping)

1 recipe Sub Roll Croutons (page 68)

instructions

1 Prepare Sub Roll Croutons and set aside.

2 Brown beef: Heat oil in 6-quart (or larger) pot or Dutch oven over medium-high heat. In bowl, toss beef with 2 tablespoons flour, 1 teaspoon salt, 1 teaspoon black pepper, and garlic powder. Add beef mixture to oil and spread it out into an even layer on bottom of pot. Do this in batches, if necessary, so as to not overcrowd pot and cause beef to steam. Cook until beef has browned (about 5 minutes), stirring occasionally. Remove beef with slotted spoon and set aside.

3 Melt butter in pot. Add onions, celery, and garlic and cook for about 4 minutes, or until vegetables have softened a bit, stirring occasionally.

4 Sprinkle remaining ¼ cup flour on top of onion mixture. Stir to coat and continue stirring for 1 to 2 minutes while flour cooks. Gradually

pour in wine and whisk mixture quickly to fully incorporate flour into liquid until smooth. Then stir to loosen and scrape up any browned bits on bottom of pot.

5 Add broth, mushrooms, Worcestershire and hot sauces, remaining ½ teaspoon salt, and ½ teaspoon black pepper and stir until all ingredients are well combined. Cover pot and bring mixture to a simmer. Simmer, uncovered, for about 12 to 15 minutes, or until all vegetables have softened.

6 Reduce heat to low. Then purée soup until smooth using an immersion blender. Slowly whisk in cheeses, 1 cup at a time, ensuring that each cup has melted before adding the next. Add beef back to pot and cook just long enough to heat it, another 1 to 2 minutes. Turn off heat.

7 Ladle soup into bowls and top with Sub Roll Croutons and pickled peppers, if desired.

recipe notes

- It will be easier to slice the meat if it is slightly frozen.

- If you don't like mushrooms, leave them out.

- If you prefer a chunkier, brothier soup, you can skip the puréeing step.

- For a unique twist to this soup, finish cooking it like French onion soup. In place of croutons, slice rolls into thick slices and do not mix cheese into soup. Instead, ladle soup into ovenproof bowls, and top each with a slice of roll and a generous helping of cheese. Then place bowls under broiler for 1 to 2 minutes, or until cheese is melted and bubbling.

sub roll croutons

3 sub or torpedo rolls cut into ½-inch cubes
2 to 3 tablespoons olive oil
Pinch salt and black pepper

Arrange rack in middle of oven, then preheat to 375°F.

Toss cubed bread with oil. Then arrange cubes in a single layer on parchment-lined sheet pan and sprinkle with salt and pepper.

Bake bread on middle rack for about 8 to 10 minutes or until golden and crispy. Set aside, uncovered, at room temperature.

You can make these croutons 3 to 4 hours in advance and hold them, uncovered, at room temperature.

reuben soup | *Serves 4 to 6*

Of all of the soups in this book, I found this one the most challenging. Having said that, once I came up with the idea to SOUPify a Reuben sandwich, I couldn't let it go. All I could think about was "Buttery Rye Croutons" and the decision was made—I needed to figure out this soup.

I get it—a Reuben sandwich in soup form sounds a little out there or even downright strange. But you're going to have to trust me on this one. That classic flavor combination of tender corned beef, melted Swiss cheese, tangy sauerkraut, and creamy dressing in between layers of buttered and toasted rye bread is pretty darn special and comes together really well in this thick and hearty soup version. Close your eyes and you will swear that you're in a New York deli having "what she's having." Sit back, have a spoonful, and enjoy the moment.

ingredients

4 tablespoons unsalted butter

1½ cups diced yellow onion (about ¾ medium onion)

¾ cup diced celery (about 2 to 3 ribs)

½ teaspoon caraway seeds

¼ cup all-purpose flour

6 cups low-sodium beef broth

1 russet potato, cut into ¼-inch dice, held in cold water to prevent browning

2½ tablespoons ketchup

4 teaspoons spicy brown/deli mustard

4 teaspoons sweet relish

1 tablespoon prepared horseradish

2 teaspoons Worcestershire sauce

½ teaspoon salt

¼ teaspoon black pepper

12 ounces thinly sliced corned beef, leftover or from deli, chopped into bite-sized pieces

12 ounces Swiss cheese, shredded or cut into very small pieces

¾ cup sauerkraut, drained (save the brine)

1 cup sour cream

3 tablespoons sauerkraut brine

½ cup finely chopped chives

1 recipe Buttery Rye Croutons (page 71)

instructions

1 Prepare Buttery Rye Croutons and set aside.

2 Melt butter in 6-quart (or larger) pot or Dutch oven over medium heat. When butter has melted, add onions, celery, and caraway seeds. Cook for about 4 minutes or until vegetables have softened a bit, stirring occasionally.

3 Sprinkle flour on top of onion mixture. Stir to coat and continue stirring for 1 to 2 minutes while flour cooks. Gradually pour in 2 cups broth and whisk mixture quickly to fully incorporate flour into liquid until smooth. Then stir to loosen and scrape up any browned bits on bottom of pot.

4 Add remaining broth, potatoes (drain first if being held in water), ketchup, mustard, relish, horseradish, Worcestershire sauce,

salt, and black pepper. Mix until all ingredients are well combined. Cover pot and bring mixture to a simmer. Simmer, mostly covered, until potatoes are tender, stirring occasionally (about 20 to 25 minutes).

5 Reduce heat to very low and add the following ingredients one at a time, while stirring continuously: corned beef, cheese (1 cup at a time), sauerkraut, sour cream, and sauerkraut brine. Ensure that the cheese has completely melted and cook just long enough to heat everything. Add chives and turn off heat. Do not boil soup once sour cream is added to prevent curdling.

6 Ladle soup into bowls and top with Buttery Rye Croutons.

recipe note

• Pastrami and oven-roasted turkey breast are both great alternatives to the corned beef.

buttery rye croutons topping

4 to 5 tablespoons unsalted butter
3 to 4 cups day-old rye bread cut into ¾ to 1-inch cubes (about 3 to 4 slices)
Pinch salt

Melt butter in large skillet over medium heat. Add bread cubes, toss with butter to coat, then spread them out into a single layer in skillet. Brown bread cubes, rotating and browning on multiple sides. Do this in batches, if necessary.

Transfer crispy fried bread to a bowl and toss immediately with salt. Then place croutons on a paper towel in a single layer to drain.

You can make these croutons 3 to 4 hours in advance and hold them, uncovered, at room temperature.

stuffed pepper soup | *Serves 6 to 8*

Stuffed peppers are classic, old-school comfort food that, for me, have "memories of mom" written all over them. I love their classic combination of meat, rice, and veggies stuffed into a sweet pepper, then topped with cheese and baked until melty, bubbling, and delicious. But I have to be honest—they are a bit too much work for me.

This SOUPified Stuffed Pepper Soup easily solves that issue with a streamlined approach to the traditional dish. All the usual ingredients simmer together in a pot with aromatics and seasonings for a savory and super-quick weeknight meal with a wonderful depth of flavor. It's a well-balanced meal in a bowl. In fact, do I dare say that you may never find yourself stuffing an actual pepper again? Yes, I do dare.

ingredients

2 tablespoons olive oil

1 pound lean ground beef (90/10 is perfect)

2 cups diced yellow onion (about 1 medium onion)

¼ cup chopped garlic (9 to 10 cloves)

2 teaspoons salt

1 teaspoon black pepper

1 teaspoon dried oregano

1 teaspoon dried basil

¼ teaspoon crushed red pepper

¼ cup tomato paste

½ cup dry white wine, such as pinot grigio

6 cups low-sodium beef or chicken broth

1 can (14.5 ounces) diced fire-roasted or plain tomatoes

1 package (10 ounces) frozen chopped spinach, thawed and drained

½ cup white rice (3½ ounces)

1 tablespoon Worcestershire sauce

4 cups diced bell peppers (about 4 medium-sized peppers)

2 cups shredded mozzarella (about 8 ounces, for topping)

½ to ¾ cup grated Pecorino Romano cheese (for topping)

instructions

1 Brown beef: Heat oil in 6-quart (or larger) pot or Dutch oven over medium-high heat. Add beef, onions, garlic, spices, and dried herbs. Cook for about 6 to 8 minutes, or until all beef has browned. Break it up into bite-sized pieces while stirring.

2 Move beef mixture to one side of pot. Then add tomato paste and cook it for about 30 seconds. Add wine and stir to loosen and scrape up any browned bits on bottom of pot.

3 Add broth, tomatoes, spinach, rice, and Worcestershire sauce. Mix until all ingredients are well combined. Partially cover pot and bring mixture to a simmer, stirring often so that rice does not stick. Depending on the variety of rice that you use, it may take anywhere from 12 to 20 minutes until rice is mostly cooked.

4 Once rice is mostly cooked, stir in bell peppers and simmer for another 8 to 10 minutes or until peppers have softened. Turn off heat.

5 Ladle soup into bowls and top with mozzarella and Pecorino cheeses.

recipe notes

- Ground turkey and chicken are both great substitutes for the beef. For something a little different, substitute half the ground beef with hot or sweet Italian sausage.

- The cheese topping is key to the final flavor of the soup—be generous when you top off your bowl!

Reuben Soup, page 69

Chinese Egg Roll Soup, page 90

pork *soups*

twice-baked, loaded potato soup with bacon | *Serves 6 to 8*

A great example of comfort food at its most decadent, twice-baked, loaded potatoes are one of those rich dishes that we probably reserve for special occasions. Full of cheese, sour cream, butter, and bacon, they are not exactly everyday food. SOUPify them, though, and it somehow becomes acceptable to enjoy them on a more regular basis throughout the long, cold winter months.

Twice-Baked, Loaded Potato Soup with Bacon is, in all seriousness, the potato soup of your dreams. It is oh-so-creamy and cheesy and full of all the flavors and textures that we love to pile onto a comforting baked potato in soul-warming, belly-satisfying bowl form. And to top it all off (literally and figuratively), there are lots of salty and delicious Crispy Potato Skins—because "crispy potato on soft potato" should have its own bragging rights!

ingredients

12 ounces bacon cut into ½-inch strips while raw

2 cups diced yellow onion (about 1 medium onion)

1 cup chopped green onions (about 4 onions)

¼ cup chopped garlic (9 to 10 cloves)

¼ cup all-purpose flour

3 cups low-sodium vegetable or chicken broth

3 pounds russet potatoes, peeled and diced (peels reserved for Crispy Potato Skins), held in cold water to prevent browning

3 cups whole milk

2 teaspoons salt

½ teaspoon paprika

¼ teaspoon black pepper

¼ teaspoon cayenne

1 cup sour cream

1 pound sharp cheddar cheese, shredded or cut into very small pieces

½ cup finely chopped chives

1 recipe Crispy Potato Skins (page 80)

instructions

1 Peel potatoes, then prepare Crispy Potato Skins and set aside.

2 Cook bacon: Place bacon in 6-quart (or larger) pot or Dutch over medium heat. Slowly cook it until it becomes crispy and most of the fat has been rendered. Remove bacon with a slotted spoon and set it aside to drain on paper towels. Remove all but about 3 tablespoons of rendered fat from the pot and use for other purpose or discard. Leave enough fat to cover bottom of pot.

3 Add onions and garlic and cook for about 4 minutes, or until onions have softened a bit, stirring occasionally.

4 Sprinkle flour on top of onion mixture; stir to coat and continue stirring for 1 to 2 minutes while flour cooks. Gradually pour in 2 cups broth and whisk mixture quickly to fully incorporate flour into liquid until smooth.

Then stir to loosen and scrape up any browned bits on bottom of pot.

5 Add remaining broth, potatoes (drain first if being held in water), milk, salt, paprika, and black and cayenne peppers. Stir until all ingredients are well combined. Cover pot and bring mixture to a simmer. Simmer, partially covered, until potatoes are tender, stirring frequently. This could take 20 to 30 minutes. Do not boil soup once milk is added to prevent curdling.

6 Reduce heat to low. Then partially purée mixture using an immersion blender. Be sure to leave some bigger chunks as this results in a great, chunky texture. Gradually stir in sour cream, then cheese, 1 cup at a time, ensuring each cup has melted before adding the next. Finish by stirring in chives and about ¾ of reserved crispy bacon. Then turn off heat.

7 Ladle soup into bowls and top with Crispy Potato Skins and remaining bacon.

recipe notes

- Be sure to peel the potatoes first and don't forget to keep the peels for the Crispy Potato Skins!

- The best cheddar for this soup is extra-sharp cheddar, in my humble opinion.

- Feel free to omit the bacon for a vegetarian-friendly soup.

crispy potato skins

¼ to ½ cup olive oil or as needed
Potato peels from all peeled potatoes in main soup recipe
Pinch salt

Heat oil in large skillet over medium-high heat. Once oil starts to spread out and glisten, add potato peels and fry them until crispy. Use tongs to turn over peels while frying.

When peels are brown and crispy, remove them immediately with a slotted spoon and transfer them to paper towels to drain. Sprinkle them with salt immediately. Set aside, uncovered, at room temperature.

You can make these potato skins 3 to 4 hours in advance and hold them, uncovered, at room temperature.

Penne alla vodka is actually a pretty controversial dish in terms of its origins. Many swear that it is an American invention, while others insist that it appeared on menus in Italy first. Regardless, there is no doubt that this vodka- and cream-laced tomato sauce paired with chunky penne pasta has become firmly entrenched as an Italian American classic in homes and restaurants alike. There's a reason for that. IT. IS. GOOD.

As Americans, we love a good tomato soup, and we also love a good creamy pasta. So it seems logical that we should also love a creamy tomato soup that contains pasta, right? Yes, it does. Penne alla Vodka Soup is like comfort food turbo-charged—one bite will not be enough. In fact, one pot will not be enough, and you may find yourself reaching for this recipe over and over throughout soup season. Don't fight it. And don't leave out the Garlic Confit and roasted red peppers! They add a touch of sweetness to the finished soup that complements the tomatoes perfectly. And that crispy pancetta topping? It's the mic drop at the end of this delicious kitchen performance.

ingredients

12 ounces pancetta, chopped into very small pieces

2 cups diced yellow onions (about 1 medium onion)

¼ cup chopped garlic (9 to 10 cloves)

2 cups lightly packed chopped fresh basil leaves, divided

½ teaspoon crushed red pepper

½ cup tomato paste

1 cup vodka

6 cups low-sodium chicken broth

3 cans (14.5 ounces) whole or diced tomatoes

1 cup roasted red pepper, drained, no seeds (about 8 ounces)

¼ cup Garlic Confit cloves (page 112)

1 tablespoon salt

½ teaspoon black pepper

2 cups pennette (mini penne) or other small pasta such as orecchiette or ditalini (10 ounces)

1 cup heavy cream

½ cup grated Pecorino Romano cheese (optional topping)

Freshly ground black pepper (optional topping)

instructions

1 Prepare Garlic Confit if you do not have any on hand.

2 Cook pancetta: Place pancetta in 6-quart (or larger) pot or Dutch oven over medium heat. Slowly cook it until it becomes crispy and most of the fat has been rendered. (This could take 15 to 20 minutes.) Remove pancetta with slotted spoon and set it aside to drain on paper towels. Remove all but about 3 tablespoons of rendered fat from the pot and use for other purpose or discard. Leave enough fat to cover bottom of pot.

3 Add onions, garlic, 1 cup basil, and crushed red pepper. Cook for about 4 minutes, or until onions have softened a bit, stirring occasionally.

4 Move onion mixture to one side of pot. Then add tomato paste and cook it for about 30 seconds. Remove pot from heat. Then pour in vodka and stir to loosen and scrape up any browned bits on bottom of pot.

5 Return pot to heat and add broth, tomatoes, roasted peppers, Garlic Confit, salt, and black pepper. Stir until all ingredients are well combined. Cover pot and bring mixture to a simmer, stirring occasionally. Simmer, partially covered, for about 8 to 10 minutes, or until all vegetables have softened. Reduce heat to low and carefully purée mixture until smooth using an immersion blender.

6 Increase heat and return mixture to a simmer. Add pasta and stir well. Simmer until pasta is *al dente*, using instructions on pasta package as a guideline, stirring continuously so that pasta doesn't stick or get clumpy. Taste pasta along the way to monitor its doneness.

7 Once pasta is *al dente*, reduce heat to low. Then whisk in cream and cook for another 2 minutes while stirring. Add additional liquid if you want a brothier soup. Stir in ¾ of the crispy pancetta and remaining 1 cup basil, then turn off heat.

8 Ladle soup into bowls and top with remaining crispy pancetta and optional toppings, if desired.

recipe notes

- If you aren't able to find pancetta, bacon is an acceptable substitute.

- You can easily make this soup vegetarian by omitting the pancetta or low-carb by omitting the pasta.

I once read that sausage and broccoli rabe are a marriage destined to last, and I couldn't agree more. There's a reason that the classics are classic—they make perfect sense and are unwavering in their appeal. This traditional southern Italian pasta dish is a great example of that. Hailing from the seaside town of Bari, this pasta, pork, and bitter greens combination is a tribute to culinary simplicity, with so few ingredients that it can be thrown together into something delicious in a pinch.

Its SOUPified version is no exception. In one pot, Italian sausage, broccoli rabe, and bite-sized pasta come together into a warming bowl of comfort food with a little added flavor from some tomato paste and savory miso. Finish it with a generous sprinkle of sharp Pecorino Romano cheese for an additional burst of flavor.

ingredients

2 tablespoons olive oil

1 pound hot or sweet Italian sausage, casings removed

½ cup chopped garlic (18 to 20 cloves)

½ teaspoon crushed red pepper (optional)

1 tablespoon tomato paste

8 cups low-sodium chicken broth

2 large bunches broccoli rabe, ends cut off and discarded, leaves and florets chopped into bite-sized pieces, stems finely chopped (about 2 pounds)

¼ tsp salt

¼ teaspoon black pepper

2 cups orecchiette pasta (8 ounces)

3 tablespoons white miso

¾ to 1 cup Pecorino Romano cheese, plus more for topping

instructions

1 Brown sausage: Heat oil in 6-quart (or larger) pot or Dutch oven over medium-high heat. Add sausage and cook for about 6 to 8 minutes, or until it has browned. Break up sausage into bite-sized pieces while stirring.

2 Reduce heat to medium. Then add garlic and crushed red pepper and cook for about 3 minutes, stirring regularly to prevent burning.

3 Move sausage mixture to one side of pot. Then add tomato paste and cook it for about 30 seconds. Add 2 cups broth and stir to loosen and scrape up any browned bits on bottom of pot.

4 Add remaining broth, broccoli rabe, salt, and black pepper and stir until all ingredients are well combined. Cover pot and bring mixture to a boil. Then add pasta and stir well. Boil until pasta is *al dente*, using instructions on pasta package as a guideline, stirring

continuously so that pasta doesn't stick or get clumpy. Taste pasta along the way to monitor its doneness.

5 Once pasta is *al dente*, reduce heat to low and whisk in miso. Stir until miso is well incorporated into broth. Add additional liquid if you want a brothier soup.

6 Turn off heat, add cheese, and stir until melted. Add more or less cheese based on your personal preference.

7 Ladle soup into bowls and top with additional Pecorino Romano cheese, if desired.

recipe notes

• Use any kind of Italian sausage in this recipe—from mild to spicy, to chicken or turkey—based on your preference.

• If you are unable to find miso, you can use 1½ tablespoons low-sodium soy sauce.

• Salt to taste as the miso and cheese add so much that you might not need any.

sausage and pepper soup | *Serves 4 to 6*

If I had to pick one sandwich that was most representative of the entire Italian American community, it would no doubt be sausage and peppers on a soft sub roll. Ubiquitous at street markets and fairs across the country, at backyard cookouts and at game-day parties everywhere, this pork and pepper pairing leaves no palate (or belly) unsatisfied.

This SOUPified version of the popular combo comes together quickly for a hearty and filling weeknight meal. With lots of onions, garlic, and tomato complementing the rich Italian sausage, this simple, brothy soup recipe is bursting with flavor and texture, just like its non-bowl cousin. In fact, you may just find yourself grabbing a sub roll to go along with it!

ingredients

2 tablespoons olive oil

2 pounds hot or sweet Italian sausage, casings removed

2 cups diced yellow onion (about 1 medium onion)

¼ cup chopped garlic (9 to 10 cloves)

⅛ teaspoon crushed red pepper

1½ cups dry white wine, such as pinot grigio

3 cups low-sodium chicken broth

1 can (28 ounces) diced fire-roasted or plain tomatoes

½ teaspoon salt

¼ teaspoon black pepper

5 cups diced bell peppers (about 5 medium-sized peppers)

½ cup chopped fresh basil

1 cup grated Pecorino Romano cheese (optional topping)

instructions

1 Brown sausage: In 6-quart (or larger) pot or Dutch oven, heat oil over medium-high heat. Add sausage and cook for about 6 to 8 minutes, or until it has browned. Break up sausage into bite-sized pieces while stirring.

2 Reduce heat to medium. Then add onions, garlic, and crushed red pepper. Cook for about 4 minutes, or until onions have softened a bit, stirring occasionally.

3 Pour in wine and stir to loosen and scrape up any browned bits on the bottom of pot.

4 Add broth, tomatoes, salt, and black pepper. Stir until all ingredients are well combined. Partially cover pot and bring mixture to a simmer, stirring occasionally. Add bell peppers and continue to simmer, partially

covered, for 10 to 12 minutes or until all vegetables have softened. Turn heat off and stir in basil.

5 Ladle soup into bowls and top with Pecorino Romano cheese, if desired.

recipe note

- Use any kind of Italian sausage in this recipe— from mild to spicy, to chicken or turkey— based on your preference.

chinese egg roll soup | *Serves 6 to 8*

I love this soup! I love it more than I ever thought that I could love a bowl version of something crispy, salty and fried (my Achilles' heel). It is so surprisingly like a classic Chinese egg roll, especially once topped with the Crispy Wontons, that you may find yourself reaching for the duck sauce and Chinese mustard. That is actually not a bad plan, to be honest, as I think both of those condiments go really well drizzled on this Chinese Egg Roll Soup!

This SOUPified Chinese Egg Roll is a warming and comforting dish that does not disappoint. It's full of flavor and texture, nutritious with loads of vegetables, and completely customizable to boot! Make it your own with all pork, all chicken, all shrimp, or all veggies. I happen to love the classic Asian pairing of pork and shrimp, and so that is what I have presented here. Whatever you do, though, don't leave out that final drizzle of toasted sesame oil—it is magical and makes the soup downright irresistible.

Chinese Food Night will never be the same.

ingredients

2 tablespoons olive oil

1 pound ground pork

2 cups diced yellow onion (about 1 medium onion)

1 cup diced celery (about 3 to 4 ribs)

1 heaping cup shredded carrot (about 4 ounces)

¼ cup chopped garlic (9 to 10 cloves)

2 tablespoons grated fresh ginger or 1½ teaspoon ground ginger

⅛ teaspoon crushed red pepper

1¼ pounds thinly shredded or chopped green cabbage (about 1 small cabbage; see Recipe Note, page 92)

8 cups low-sodium chicken broth

1 cup low-sodium soy sauce

½ teaspoon salt

¼ teaspoon black pepper

½ teaspoon Chinese five spice (optional)

8 ounces shrimp, peeled, deveined, tail off, cut into bite-sized pieces

1 cup diced red bell pepper (about 1 medium-sized pepper)

8 ounces shiitake mushrooms, stems discarded, caps sliced very thinly (about 3 cups sliced)

1 cup chopped green onion (about 4 onions)

2 teaspoons toasted sesame oil

¼ cup white sesame seeds (optional garnish)

1 recipe Crispy Wontons (page 92) or 1½ cups store-bought crispy wonton strips

instructions

1 Prepare Crispy Wontons (if using) and set aside.

2 Brown pork: Heat oil in 6-quart (or larger) pot or Dutch oven over medium-high heat. Add pork and cook for about 6 to 8 minutes, or until it has lightly browned. Break up pork into bite-sized pieces while stirring. Remove pork to separate plate using a slotted spoon. Set aside.

3 Add onions, celery, carrots, garlic, ginger, and crushed red pepper. Cook for about 4 minutes, or until vegetables have softened a bit, stirring occasionally. Add cabbage and continue to cook another 2 minutes while stirring.

4 Add 2 cups broth and stir to loosen and scrape up any browned bits on bottom of pot.

5 Add remaining broth, soy sauce, salt, black pepper, and Chinese five spice (if using). Stir until all ingredients are well combined. Partially cover pot and bring mixture to a simmer, stirring occasionally. Simmer, partially covered, about 8 to 10 minutes, or until all vegetables have softened.

6 Stir in shrimp, bell peppers, mushrooms, green onions, and reserved pork. Continue to simmer, uncovered, until the shrimp are fully cooked (about 2 to 3 minutes). Turn off heat, drizzle in sesame oil, and stir well.

7 Ladle soup into bowls and top with Crispy Wontons (or wonton strips) and sesame seeds, if desired.

recipe notes

- For the shredded cabbage, I encourage you to find and use a prepared coleslaw kit. It saves so much time! But find one that doesn't include red cabbage.

- If you don't have low-sodium soy sauce, cut the amount by 25% and consider not adding any salt.

- Chinese five spice is optional, but use it if you already have it in your pantry. It adds an interesting, earthy flavor to the finished soup as it contains cinnamon, anise seed, cloves, ginger, and fennel seed.

- Drizzle this soup with some sriracha or Chinese mustard if you'd like some heat!

crispy wontons

5 egg roll or 20 wonton wrappers sliced into thin strips
1-2 cups vegetable oil or as needed for frying
Salt

Heat oil in large skillet over medium-high heat. Once oil starts to spread out and glisten, add sliced egg roll or wonton wrappers and fry them until brown and crispy. Use tongs to turn over strips while frying. Work quickly as they brown very fast!

Remove fried wontons with tongs or slotted spoon and transfer them to paper towels to drain. Sprinkle with salt immediately. Set aside, uncovered, at room temperature.

You can make these Crispy Wontons a couple of hours in advance and hold them, uncovered, at room temperature.

Twice-Baked, Loaded Potato Soup with Bacon, page 78

Proscuitto and Melon Soup, page 99

cold *soups*

caprese soup | *Serves 6 to 8*

Is there any more recognizable Italian summer salad than the caprese? The classic combination of sweet tomatoes, creamy fresh mozzarella cheese, and fragrant basil drizzled with extra-virgin olive oil is arguably one of the world's most popular combinations. I admit that it absolutely does not need any changes, improvements, or second editions. So I like to think of this cold Caprese Soup as an alternative way to enjoy the beautiful flavors that we all know and love.

Cold soups are a great way to start a light summer meal and an easy way to add a fun dimension to lunch or dinner. This SOUPified Caprese is easy and quick to prepare, making it an ideal starter. Purée sweet grape tomatoes, basil, and a little raw garlic with a fair amount of sweet Garlic Confit, and lots of fruity extra-virgin olive oil. Add a splash of fresh lemon juice and vinegar to round out and fortify the simple flavors in this dish. Hand-pulled strands of fresh mozzarella top it all off and complete the experience. Feel free to serve this with some rustic pane di casa Italian bread and a glass of your favorite vino!

ingredients

3 pints red grape or cherry tomatoes

3 cups lightly packed fresh basil

2 raw garlic cloves

2 cans (14.5 ounces) diced, cherry, or baby Roma tomatoes

4 tablespoons Garlic Confit cloves (page 112)

4 teaspoons fresh lemon juice

2 teaspoons red wine vinegar

2 teaspoons salt or to taste

½ teaspoon black pepper

½ teaspoon crushed red pepper

1 cup extra-virgin olive oil

6 to 8 ounces fresh mozzarella, pulled by hand into small, bite-sized pieces (for topping)

Lemon oil or balsamic glaze (optional topping)

instructions

1 Prepare and cool Garlic Confit if you do not have any on hand.

2 Combine fresh tomatoes, basil, and raw garlic in bowl of a large food processor or blender. Blend until chopped well (about 20 seconds).

3 Add canned tomatoes, Garlic Confit, lemon juice, vinegar, salt, black pepper, and crushed red pepper. Continue to purée until smooth while carefully drizzling in oil. Do this in batches, if necessary, and use a spatula to scrape down sides, ensuring that all ingredients are fully incorporated. Add salt to taste and blend again.

4 Transfer soup to a bowl, cover it tightly with plastic wrap, and chill until serving. You can serve it either chilled or at room temperature.

5 Ladle soup into bowls. Top each with a few pieces of fresh mozzarella and a drizzle of lemon oil or balsamic glaze, if desired.

recipe notes

- Depending on the size of your food processor, you may need to make this recipe in batches to prevent overflowing. If you are making it in batches, combine the multiple batches in a large bowl, and mix well.

- Note that the raw garlic flavor in this soup becomes much stronger over time, so reduce the amount of garlic to your taste, especially if you will be eating this soup the day after you make it.

- This soup is best made and served on the same day, but you can still serve it on the second day. Do not freeze.

- As it sits, the soup may separate, so give it a quick stir before serving if necessary.

prosciutto and melon soup | *Serves 6 to 8*

There's a reason prosciutto and melon go so well together and are enjoyed up and down the Italian peninsula. It's that classic flavor marriage of salty and sweet that shouldn't seem to work, but magically and deliciously does. Without getting too scientific, this pairing works because of flavor layering. Salt is a flavor enhancer, and so it enhances the flavor of the sugar. In the right proportions, your brain receives a positive biological response. In other words, the salty prosciutto makes the sweet cantaloupe taste even better than on its own, and therefore, you become happy. Really happy.

Whatever the reason, I can't get enough of this duo. And therefore, I had to SOUPify it. The result is a refreshing, chilled melon soup with a salty, crispy topping that is impressive enough to be served as a starter for a formal dinner party, but casual enough to pair with your green salad on a hot summer afternoon. A heavenly proposition!

ingredients

2 cantaloupes (about 3 pounds each), rinsed under cold water, peeled, seeded, fibers removed, cut into 1- to 2-inch chunks

¾ cup nonfat Greek yogurt

4 tablespoons fresh lime juice

3 tablespoons sherry vinegar

2 tablespoons extra-virgin olive oil

1¼ teaspoons salt

½ cup lightly packed chopped fresh mint (for topping)

1 recipe Crispy Prosciutto (page 101)

instructions

1 Prepare Crispy Prosciutto and set aside.

2 Place the following ingredients in bowl of a large food processor or blender: cantaloupe chunks, yogurt, lime juice, vinegar, olive oil, and salt. Blend about 60 seconds, or until all ingredients are fully puréed. Do this in batches, if necessary, and use a spatula to scrape down sides, ensuring that all ingredients are fully incorporated.

3 Transfer soup to a bowl and cover it tightly with plastic wrap. Chill soup for at least 1 hour before serving.

4 Ladle soup into bowls and top with a few pieces of Crispy Prosciutto and chopped mint.

recipe notes

- Depending on the size of your food processor, you may need to make this recipe in batches to prevent overflowing. If making it in batches, combine the multiple batches in a large bowl, and mix well.

- This soup is best made and served on the same day, but you can still serve it on the second day. Do not freeze.

- As it sits, the soup may separate, so give it a quick stir before serving if necessary.

- This soup is best when it is chilled well! Be sure to let it spend at least 1 hour in the refrigerator before serving.

crispy prosciutto

12 to 16 slices thinly sliced prosciutto (about ⅓ to ½ pound)

Arrange rack in middle of oven and preheat to 350°F.

Carefully arrange prosciutto slices in a single layer on a parchment-lined sheet pan. Roast on middle rack until crispy (about 12 to 15 minutes).

Transfer to paper towels to drain and cool, then crumble into smaller pieces. Set aside at room temperature, uncovered.

You can make this topping 2 to 3 hours in advance and hold it, uncovered, at room temperature.

greek salad soup | *Serves 6 to 8*

Greek salad that you can eat with a spoon? Yes.

Soup that can replace your salad? Indeed.

I never thought it was possible, but I am now convinced that the options for SOUPification are endless. Inspired by the simple technique used to make chilled Spanish gazpacho, this cold Greek Salad Soup is one-of-a-kind. Containing all the signature flavors of the diner classic, it's nutritious, delicious, refreshing, and easy to prepare. This soup is a perfect lunch on a warm spring day, or a unique side to a grilled steak or shrimp dinner. Eat it before or after the rest of your meal (just like a green salad). You will be surprised at how much this soup tastes like the original!

ingredients

1½ pounds ripe tomatoes, cored and cut into 1 to 2-inch pieces

1½ pounds cucumber, peeled and seeded (see instructions for different cuts)

1 large green bell pepper, cored and seeded (see instructions for different cuts)

1 medium red onion, peeled (see instructions for different cuts)

2 tablespoons extra-virgin olive oil

2 tablespoons red wine vinegar

2 tablespoons Garlic Confit cloves (page 112)

¼ cup pitted Kalamata olives, divided

¼ cup fresh oregano, leaves only

1 tablespoon fresh lemon juice

1 raw garlic clove

1 teaspoon salt

¼ teaspoon black pepper

1 cup crumbled feta cheese (for topping)

2 teaspoons capers, drained (for topping)

pita chips, for serving (optional)

instructions

1 Prepare and cool Garlic Confit if you do not have any on hand.

2 Prep cucumber, bell pepper, and onion as follows: cut about one-third of each vegetable into ¼-inch diced pieces and set aside. You can cut the remaining two-thirds of each vegetable into large chunks because you will be puréeing them.

3 Place the following ingredients in bowl of a large food processor or blender: tomatoes; large chunks of cucumber, bell pepper, and red onion; olive oil, vinegar, Garlic Confit, 2 tablespoons olives, oregano, lemon juice, raw garlic clove, salt, and black pepper. Blend about 60 seconds, or until all ingredients are fully puréed. Do this in batches, if necessary, and use a spatula to scrape down sides, ensuring that all ingredients are fully incorporated.

4 Transfer mixture to a bowl. Then stir in the re-served ¼-inch cuts of cucumber, bell pepper, and red onion. Cover bowl with plastic wrap. Then chill soup for at least 1 hour before serving.

5 Ladle soup into bowls and top with feta cheese, capers, and remaining olives. Serve with pita chips, if desired.

recipe notes

- This recipe was designed to have both puréed and chunky textures. However, if you are short on time and are not that concerned with texture, feel free to purée all of the cucumber, bell pepper, and red onion for a fully puréed soup.

- Select high quality, juicy tomatoes with a fair amount of flesh for this recipe. Vine-ripened, heirloom, and beefsteak tomatoes work well. And use your best extra-virgin olive oil for this recipe!

- Depending on the size of your food processor, you may need to make this recipe in batches to prevent overflowing. If making it in batches, combine the multiple batches in a large bowl, and mix well.

- This soup is best made and served on the same day, but you can still serve it on the second day. Do not freeze.

- As it sits, the soup may separate, so give it a quick stir before serving if necessary.

- This soup is best when it is chilled well! Be sure to let it spend at least 1 hour in the refrigerator before serving.

guacamole soup | *Serves 4 to 6*

I admit that this chilled Guacamole Soup may push the boundaries between "soup" and "dip." But I am okay with that.

I have always maintained that guacamole is one of the few perfect foods out there. It is creamy, nutritious, delightfully salty, and universally loved, making it an ideal candidate for SOUPification, in my humble opinion.

Like the original, this chilled Guacamole Soup is tasty, filling, and versatile. It has an amazing, super-bright, light green color that would look just gorgeous (and taste great, of course) topped with grilled shrimp. It also doubles as a dressing or a light dip and is just perfect on steak tacos or paired with a crudité platter.

Compared to the dish that inspired it, the SOUPified version is lightened up a bit, so you can eat it with a spoon. It makes a lovely starter to a light meal and is season-proof—it works in both hot and cold weather! ¡Buen provecho!

ingredients

1 medium yellow onion, cut into 1-inch pieces

3 serrano peppers, stemmed, cut in half, seeds of 1 pepper only (or more if you like a lot of heat!)

¼ cup cilantro leaves

4 teaspoons lime zest

1 tablespoon minced raw garlic (about 3 cloves)

Pulp of 3 ripe avocados

1½ cups nonfat plain Greek yogurt

½ cup fresh lime juice (zest limes first)

3 tablespoons Garlic Confit cloves (page 112)

2 tablespoons extra-virgin olive oil

1½ to 2 cups cold water

2 teaspoons salt or to taste

1 cup diced fresh tomatoes (for topping)

Tortilla chips, for serving (optional)

instructions

1 Prepare and cool Garlic Confit if you do not have any on hand.

2 Combine onion, serrano pepper, cilantro, lime zest, and raw garlic in bowl of a large food processor or blender and blend until chopped well.

3 Add avocado pulp, yogurt, lime juice, Garlic Confit, and olive oil. Continue to blend until all ingredients are fully incorporated.

4 Add water, ½ cup at a time, and purée until mixture is completely smooth (60 to 90 seconds). Do this in batches, if necessary, and use a spatula to scrape down sides, ensuring that all ingredients are fully incorporated. If mixture is still a little thick after adding 1½ cups water, add the last ½ cup. Add salt to taste and blend again.

5 Transfer soup to a bowl and cover it tightly with plastic wrap. Chill soup for at least 1 hour before serving.

6 Ladle soup into bowls, top with tomatoes, and serve with tortilla chips, if desired.

recipe notes

- Be sure to zest the limes before squeezing out their juice!

- The avocado pulp should be soft and creamy so that it blends easily.

- Depending on the size of your food processor, you may need to make this recipe in batches to prevent overflowing. If making it in batches, combine the multiple batches in a large bowl, and mix well.

- Note that the raw garlic flavor in this soup becomes much stronger over time, so reduce the amount of garlic to your personal taste, especially if you will be eating this soup on the day after you make it.

- This soup is best made and served on the same day, but you can still serve it on the second day. Do not freeze.

- As it sits, the soup may separate, so give it a quick stir before serving if necessary.

- This soup is best when it is chilled well! Be sure to let it spend at least 1 hour in the refrigerator before serving.

Garlic Confit and Garlic Oil, page 112

supporting recipes

basic homemade stock | *Makes About 1 Gallon*

Nothing can replace the rich flavor, simplicity, and versatility of homemade stock. While it may be more of a time commitment than you are willing to make on a weekday, try it out one weekend and see what you think. My guess is that you will start stockpiling your residual meat bones in the freezer out of the pure satisfaction that only making your own homemade stock can give you!

ingredients

6 to 8 pounds chicken or beef bones, rinsed

1½ gallons cold water

1 pound yellow onions cut into quarters

8 ounces celery ribs with leaves cut into 1- to 2-inch pieces

8 ounces carrots, cut into 1- to 2-inch pieces

1 lemon, cut into quarters, or ¾ cup dry white wine

4 parsley stems

2 bay leaves

¼ teaspoon black peppercorns

¼ teaspoon dried thyme

instructions

1 Rinse bones to remove blood and excess fat.

2 Place all ingredients in a large stock pot or Dutch oven. Bring the water to a boil over high heat. Once it reaches a boil, turn the heat down immediately to medium-low or lower, until the mixture remains at a light simmer. Simmer, uncovered, for 5 to 6 hours (for chicken stock) or 6 to 8 hours (for beef stock), skimming any scum that forms along the way.

3 Strain the stock using a colander and/or cheesecloth.

4 Cool the stock as quickly as possible. Store it in the refrigerator for up to 5 days or in the freezer for up to 3 months.

recipe notes

• The best bones for chicken stock are from the neck and back. The best bones for beef stock are from the back, neck, and shank and should be cut into small pieces, approximately 3 to 4 inches long, so that they can release as much flavor as possible during the cooking process. Either ask your butcher or use a meat cleaver to cut the bones.

• For a browner and more intensely flavored stock, place the unrinsed bones on a parchment-lined sheet pan in a single layer. Roast them in a 375°F oven for about 1 hour, rotating them once during the cooking process. The bones should be thoroughly browned, but not burnt. Transfer the roasted bones from the sheet pan to the stock pot and continue with the recipe above.

• It is not necessary to peel the carrots, celery, or onions.

garlic confit and garlic oil | *Makes About 1½ Cups*

This recipe is life changing. Okay, I may be exaggerating a bit, but it will, indeed, forever change your kitchen. It definitely changed mine. From the first time that I made it, in a twenty-pound batch at work, to yesterday's one-cup batch at home, it has remained the most important ingredient in my culinary arsenal and one that I always have on hand.

What is confit? It's a French word that literally means "to preserve." In cooking, it refers to food that is cooked slowly over a long period of time in oil or its own fat, such as duck or chicken confit. Often incorrectly referred to as roasted garlic, Garlic Confit is fabulous for so many reasons. It softens and sweetens the sharp flavor of garlic and makes the garlic clove mashable, spreadable, and easy to add to lots of recipes. As a bonus, it creates an abundantly flavorful, residual garlic oil that could be easily compared to the nectar of the gods!

And it couldn't be easier to make! It is basically peeled garlic cloves that have been gently and slowly heated in lots of good-quality olive oil until they transform into something silky, sweet, and mellow. I use this confit in so many dishes—garlic bread, salad dressings, puréed into sauces, just shmeared on rustic bread with some coarse salt, and in several SOUPified recipes. Its flavor is key, often balancing out the sharpness of others.

Make lots of it. Use daily.

ingredients

3 whole heads of garlic, cloves separated
and peeled (about 1 cup peeled garlic
cloves)

1 to 2 cups extra-virgin olive oil, or as needed

2 to 3 bay leaves (optional)

instructions

1 Place cloves in small or medium saucepan and pour in enough oil to completely cover them. Add bay leaves, if using.

2 Heat mixture over medium heat. Bring oil to the lightest simmer, then reduce heat to as low as possible. Continue to cook mixture over very low heat until garlic is very tender, but not falling apart. It should be only lightly browned. To test the garlic, pierce one clove with the tip of a sharp knife—it should meet with little to no resistance and be easily smashable. This could take about 30 to 45 minutes. Stir occasionally.

3 Remove pan from heat and immediately transfer confit to a clean jar or glass container. Cool Garlic Confit to room temperature, then cover jar or container tightly and promptly refrigerate it. Store in refrigerator and use within 2 to 3 weeks. Do not freeze.

recipe notes

• You can also make Garlic Confit in your oven. Preheat oven to 350°F. Combine all ingredients in small baking dish, making sure to include enough oil so that cloves are fully covered. Place baking dish on sheet pan (to accommodate any spills), then bake on middle rack until cloves are softened (about 45 minutes). Remove, cool and store in a clean, airtight container in refrigerator. Use within 2 to 3 weeks.

• As a flavor variation, add crushed red pepper, black peppercorns, fresh rosemary, or thyme sprigs to oil to cook along with garlic. Remove large pieces before refrigerating.

outtakes | *SOUPified* and the City

This cookbook came to life while I was quarantined during the COVID-19 pandemic in my New York City apartment. I wanted to provide a behind-the-scenes glimpse into cooking and photographing these *SOUPified* creations.

Though I have been developing menus and recipes for a couple of decades, I am neither a professional food photographer nor a food or prop stylist. But, I really wanted to create this cookbook so that I could share these recipes and stories with the world. And so, I trudged forward and embraced my inner scrappiness.

I did all the food photography and styling in this book. I learned along the way. In a corner of my apartment that gets some natural light for a few hours each day, I balanced bowls of soup, garnish, and props galore on top of books, cardboard, and my trusty ottoman in order to capture the spirit of my creations. It was fun in a "New York State of Mind" kind of way.

Here is *SOUPified*, behind the scenes.

index

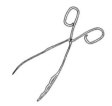

acknowledgments

To thank everyone, both those who helped in a direct, lend-a-hand kind of way and those who were just there to nurture and encourage me along this first cookbook journey, is really difficult! But, first and foremost, I would like to thank all of my friends and family who have put up with my endless chatter about *"SOUPifying"* and "the e-book" for the past several months.

And specifically, I would like to extend my appreciation:

• To my New York City and South Jersey neighbors, friends and friends-of-friends who eagerly received and consumed numerous containers of soup over and over and gave me constructive feedback in return.

• To my recipe testers—thank you for your enthusiasm, time, detail, and thoroughness! Amanda Focke, Anne LaVallee, Christine Mauro, Danielle Ferrante, Diana Racobaldo, Elizabeth Van der Wel, Erik and Karyn Librader, Gary Osifchin, Heidi and Jeff Franchetti, Holly Brandt, Jeff Staadt, Jennifer Cesa, John Celeste, Julia Obici, Lisa Glover, Lisa Grant, Martin Bates, Nicole Griffin, Octavio Martinez, Rose Leopold, and Zoe Heineman.

• To Jeff Staadt—for letting me intrude on your beachside kitchen with my recipe development and photography arsenal when I needed a change of scenery.

• To my closest friends and cheerleaders in everything life, career, and food—your ongoing encouragement and insight is invaluable! Special shout-outs to The Georgetown 6 (Liz, Claire, Mandy, Anne, Denise), Dean, Gina, Liz S., Lisa, Jeff, Sue, Angela, Octavio, Missey, Katherine and Jen, and to the many more not listed here.

• To Mary Giuliani—thank you for inviting me on your Instagram Live, where I first announced out loud that I was working on a book, thereby becoming immediately accountable to myself and others to see it through! And most of all, thank you for writing my Foreword and being forever a part of my book through your lovely words.

- To my faithful and detail-oriented editors, Claire Haddad and Liz DiMichele—thank you for working tirelessly on my manuscript and for caring so darn much about the details.

- To my designer and friend, Lizanne Hart—thank you for agreeing to go along with me on this journey and for bringing my words and photos to life on these beautiful pages!

- Most of all, I would like to thank my sister Roseanne, who has stood by me through every stage of my career change, cooking school, years of working in the industry, creating *Mangia With Michele*, and this cookbook project…opening up her home to me, my pots, my bags of tools, and all my photo props when I just had to leave the city during lockdown, but still had to make progress on the recipes, and whose clever brain came up with the title, *SOUPified*, which will forever now be part of popular culinary jargon.

From the bottom of my heart, THANK YOU.

about the author

Michele Di Pietro is an entrepreneur, chef, culinary consultant, food writer, blogger, and creator of *Mangia With Michele*, the expression of her lifelong passion for Italian ingredients, foods, recipes, culture, and traditions. She was raised in an Italian American family in southern New Jersey, where her culinary education began with a collection of relatives as teachers in a household where food and cooking were central, daily household activities. With both Sicilian and Abruzzese roots, Michele experienced distinctive, regional cuisines of Italy in an American setting while growing up, and fell in love with the act of giving of herself through preparing food for others. On Sunday mornings, Michele could be found in the kitchen cooking eggs with her mother as young as age 5, and many an afternoon was spent with her grandmother making traditional Italian comfort foods, including fresh pasta, gnocchi, and homemade "gravy."

Michele, a graduate of Georgetown University and The Restaurant School at Walnut Hill College, started out her professional career as a Certified Public Accountant at a top New York City firm, but eventually found her true calling as she worked and traveled in Europe, experiencing some of the world's finest cuisines. She left the financial world for the professional kitchen and, once fully immersed in the food industry, quickly discovered that her knowledge of numbers and CPA skills came in handy for recipe development and culinary project management. Michele eventually grew into her dream job overseeing all things culinary at the world's largest natural foods retailer, where she became an award-winning, seasoned food professional . . . until she decided to strike out on her own. She is the founder of *It's All About The Food*, where you can find her consulting on culinary strategy and menu development for an eclectic lineup of food businesses.

Throughout her busy professional culinary life, Michele has also always been an avid home cook with strong ties to her Italian roots. She is most happy and satisfied when cooking for, and breaking bread with, family and friends. It is these ties and sentiments, along with her passion for sharing both food and travel experiences with others, that led her to create *Mangia With Michele*.

She lives in Manhattan and believes that the best way to get to know people is through food—ideally, around the kitchen table.

Find her at mangiawithmichele.com and follow her at @mangiawithmichele on social channels.

Photo by Matt Carr Photography

CPSIA information can be obtained
at www.ICGtesting.com
Printed in the USA
BVHW021752061021
618127BV00010B/143